I0068231

The Piggy Banker

A Raise Creative Investors Money Journal

JACKIE MCCARTHY

Copyrighted Material

The Piggy Banker
A Raise Creative Investors Money Journal

Copyright © 2019 by Raise Creative Kidz. All Rights Reserved.

No part of this publication may be reproduced, stored in a retrieval system or transmitted, in any form or by any means – electronic, mechanical, photocopying, recording or otherwise – without prior written permission from the publisher, except for the inclusion of brief quotations in a review.

For information about this title, to order other books and/or electronic media, as well as accompanying products, or to inquire about speaker workshops or speaking engagements, contact the publisher:

Jackie@RaiseCreativeKidz.com
Raise Creative Kidz
Raise Creative Investors
http://RaiseCreativeKidz.com
http://RaiseCreativeInvestors.com
www.facebook.com/RaiseCreativeInvestors

ISBN: 978-0-9907840-2-9

Printed in the United States of America

Cover and Interior design: Raise Creative Kidz
Editing: Bailey and Kevin McCarthy

Table of Contents

How To Use *The Piggy Banker*

At <u>Raise Creative Investors</u>, our purpose is to help kids and teens increase their financial literacy knowledge. This journal starts off with information designed to teach you more about acquiring, spending and saving money. The rest of the journal contains your weekly Piggy Banker Money Journal worksheets, a place for you to keep track of your money, as well as your spending and savings habits. Below is a snapshot of The Piggy Banker Money Journal — the left chart is your **SPENDING ACCOUNT** and the right chart is your **SAVINGS ACCOUNT.** (Your money journal worksheets can be found starting on Page 24.) You will also need 3 letter-sized envelopes. Mark your first envelope: SPEND; second envelope: SHARE; and the third envelope: SAVE/Piggy Bank. Keep them together in. a box or drawer.

The Piggy Banker Money Journal   Week: _____

Starting TOTAL: Spending Account	$
MONEY IN:	
Allowance	$
Gift	$
Job	$
Other:	$
TOTAL IN:	$
MONEY OUT:	
Piggy Bank Deposit	$
Toys/Video Games/Apps	$
Food/Beverage	$
Entertainment	$
Personal Items	$
For School	$
For Car	$
Other	$
SHARE/Donate:	$
Loan to:	$
TOTAL OUT:	$

PIGGY BANK Savings Account	
Current Piggy Bank:	$
+ Money IN:	+ $
- Money OUT:	- $
= New Piggy Bank:	= $

Starting Total	$
+ TOTAL IN	+ $
- TOTAL OUT	- $
= New TOTAL put at top of next journal	= $

The Piggy Banker

A Raise Creative Investors Money Journal

Keeping Track of Your Money

The earlier you learn how to keep track of your money, the better you will be at it when you're older.

The Piggy Banker will help you keep track of the money you save, the money you spend, and help you reach the goals you have for your money. You will learn tips on ways to increase your "income" and how to decide which purchases are "wants" and which ones are "needs." This journal will also serve to get you in the habit of saving for future goals and explain the value of charitable giving.

What should I do with my money?

Piggy Bank

Historically, the Piggy Bank has served as an instructional tool to teach the basics of thrift and savings to children. The Piggy Banker will instruct you to view your "Savings" as you would money in a Piggy Bank.

Money: EARN IT

You will begin with all the money you currently have, your Starting Amount – you will need to decide how much of it you want to start your SPENDING Account with and how much you want to start your SAVINGS Account with. You will continue to accumulate money over time. Ongoing Money IN can come from a number of different sources.

Starting Amount   *Allowance*   *GIFTS*

JOBS   *Rewards*

STARTING AMOUNT

Before you start filling out your Piggy Banker Money Journal worksheets, you want to gather up all the money you have so far. You will add up all of this money (you can use a calculator or ask a parent) and this will be the basis of your first "Starting TOTAL" and your first "Current PIGGY BANK." Once you've gathered up all your starting money, decide what you want to put in the envelopes you marked "SPEND" (which is the money you can use on purchases or donations) and "SAVE/Piggy Bank" (which is the money you are saving up for a larger purchase). We will cover more about your Piggy Bank Savings Account on Page 14.

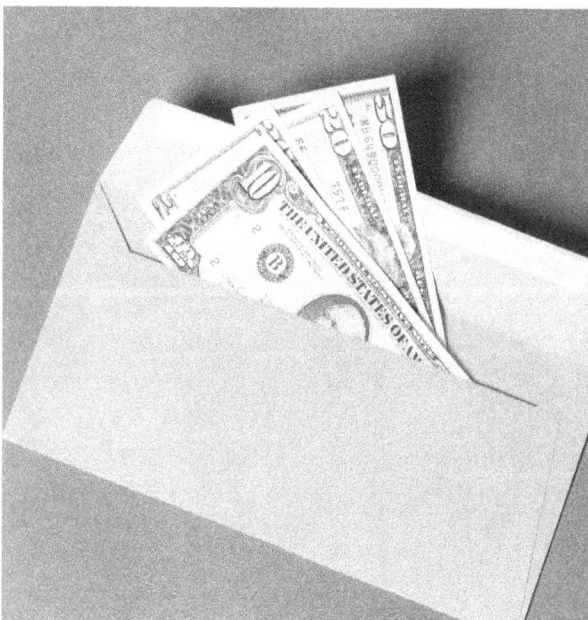

Where to Look for Money:

- Your wallet
- An old piggy bank
- In your desk drawer
- In your pockets
- Any gift cards you have
- Ask if you can gather up any change you can find in the couch or car
- Maybe ask for a starting donation from your parents (a gift)

Allowance

An Allowance (or a Commission) is an amount of money given usually to a child from his/her parents during a period of time (monthly or weekly). Often, it is given to the child for doing specific chores around the house. It can be broken down by chore or it can be a set amount.

If your parents don't give you an allowance and you want to start the conversation with them, here are a few current trends you can share with them from a new survey from RoosterMoney of 30,000 4-14 year old kids in the U.S.. Keep in mind the ultimate decision depends on what's best for your family.

1. 69% of parents surveyed gave their kids a regular allowance in 2018.

2. The average weekly allowance reported for 2018 was $9.00, which is about $470 a year.

3. The most lucrative chores were: Washing the car, Gardening, and Cleaning your room.

Children are picking up lasting money habits as young as 7 years old and setting up a consistent allowance is a great way to build positive money habits early on.

Top EARNING Chores (survey average)

1) Washing the Car, $4.60

2) Gardening, $4.34

3) Cleaning Bedroom, $2.71

4) Mopping the Floor, $2.33

5) Cleaning the Bathroom, $1.82

6) Cleaning the Kitchen, $1.72

7) Vacuuming, $1.52

8) Helping with Dinner, $1.52

9) Dusting, $1.52

10) Looking after Pets, $1.48

Earned Income – A Job

Having a part-time job will teach you good work habits that will help you in school and later on when you are ready for a full-time job. It is also a way to earn money. Many states require work permits or proof-of-age certificates for a minor to be employed, so you should check your state's Department of Labor website for that information. However, there are many smaller or one-off jobs that you usually don't need working papers for, such as:

1) Babysitting

2) Pet sitting

3) Dog walking

4) Water plants when neighbor is away

5) Lemonade stand

6) Yard work

7) Delivering newspapers

8) Help with family business

9) Summer camp counselor-in-training

10) Mother's helper for a new mom

11) Have a garage sale

12) Help clean a neighbor's garage

13) Errands for the elderly

14) Hold a car wash

15) Golf caddying

Become an Entrepreneur

It's never too young to start your own business. In fact, according to the new survey by RoosterMoney, the most entrepreneurial age is 11 years old. That age group is the most likely to boost their income by selling old toys and clothes – averaging $28 per sale.

Other business ideas that have been successful are offered services such as: dog walking, lawn mowing, snow shoveling, window washing, weeding gardens and babysitting.

GIFTS

Sometimes you may get some money put in a card for you for your birthday or holiday from friends or relatives, like grandparents. Don't be so quick to put it in your pocket, making it easier for you to spend it without thinking. Put it away and add it to your Piggy Banker Money Journal. It counts toward your "Money In" amount. Then you can be more thoughtful about whether you want to spend it quickly or save it for a larger purchase later.

For birthdays or holidays, you may also get gift cards. It might make more sense to exchange those cards with your parents for the cash equivalent. Then your parents can use the gift card, if it makes sense, and you can simply add the cash to your "Money In" amount. If you decide to keep the gift cards, still add it to your "Money In" but record it as a "GC" (gift card) and write in what store it's for. But make sure you use it when you need to, instead of cash, especially if the gift card is for a specialty store like Starbucks and you have a craving for a Frappuccino. You should always use any gift cards you have before dipping into your cash.

Also, any money your parents generously offer to give you towards the purchase of something you want, mark that down as a "Gift". If they meant it to be a loan, remember to pay them back.

OTHER: REWARDS

If you have a parent, grandparent, or other relative who gives you a few dollars as a reward for a good report card or you win money for a spelling bee contest, count that towards your "Money IN" under "OTHER". The Piggy Banker always recommends that you add it to your total money so that you can put some thought into whether you want to spend it now or save it for later.

Piggy Banker Money Journal: Money IN

The top half of your Piggy Banker Money Journal will be where you will record all your "Money IN". At the very top it will ask you for your "Starting TOTAL" for your Spending Account – this is where you will put in your "Starting Amount". At the end of each week, if you've added any new "Money IN" and/or taken any "Money OUT", you will have a "New TOTAL" amount to put at the top of the next week's worksheet.

Any money you earn from an *Allowance, Job* and any money you have received as a *Gift* you would put on the lines listed for each. If you've received any *Rewards*, you would include that under "*Other*" along with any other "Money IN" that is not included in one of the other lines, such as any loans that may have been paid back to you or any loans you may have received.

The Piggy Banker Money Journal

Starting TOTAL: Spending Account	**$**
MONEY IN:	
Allowance	$
Gift	$
Job	$
Other:	$
TOTAL IN:	$

Money: SPEND IT

Any money you want to spend should only come out of your SPEND envelope. Each time you spend money, it's important to keep track of it in *The Piggy Banker* journal. Otherwise, your money might be gone before you realize it. Also, by taking the time to write down what you spend your money on, and later reflect on it, you will be wiser about how you spend your money, which will lead to better choices going forward.

Wants versus Needs. Before you spend money on something it's good to know whether it's a Want or a Need. "Wants" are things that we would like to have but can live without. "Wants" are things like electronics, fashionable clothing (designer sneakers), toys, video games, candy/snacks, coffee drinks, or jewelry. "Needs" are things we don't have a choice on, as we may need them to survive or to carry on our basic life. "Needs" are things like basic clothing items (pants, shirts, shoes), nutritious food (milk, meat), transportation (gas, bus fare), school supplies, school sports team needs, and for our parents, things like housing, healthcare and utilities (water, heat). At your age, most of your "needs" will still be purchased by your parents, but you may start having some that you are responsible for buying or that you determine are "needs" for you.

Of course, you can spend money on things you just "Want" but you should always use your money first on the things you definitely "Need".

TOP THINGS KIDS SPEND THEIR MONEY ON (2018)

1. Candy
2. Presents
3. Books
4. Apps
5. Lego
6. Xbox
7. Pokemon
8. Roblox
9. Minecraft
10. Religious Charity

Best Price

Comparison-shopping helps you buy an item at the best available price. Do a search online to find the item at the lowest cost, including the cost of shipping. But don't just stop there, often you can find a money-off coupon you can use or activate an online money-back service.

1. For in-store COUPONS check for store fliers that come in the mail.

2. For PROMO Codes, look at internet-sites like "Coupon Cabin" and "Retail Me Not".

3. For Cash-Back on online purchases, look at activating sites like "Ebates" or "Coupon Cactus".

Value

When you are looking to buy something, you should always look at its value. What does it cost compared to what it is, its quality, and how often you would use it? If it is something that seems to cost a lot because it's trendy and the current demand is high, and yet you think you would really only use it a few times, is it really worth your money?

Also, sometimes you can find an item on-line or through Amazon that costs more in shipping than the item itself costs. Is that really a good value? Remember an item's total cost is not only its price; it is tax and shipping, too.

Finally, if available, you should read reviews on the item. Does it get good reviews, or do customers feel it's not well made, doesn't do what it says it is supposed to do, or breaks a lot? Is it a good value?

Virtual Money

Only 8% of all the money around the world is actual physical cash, the rest is money that only exists on computers. Think about how often you buy things with credit cards or on-line without actually ever seeing or touching the money used to pay for it.

When you purchase music, movies, or apps for your phone and choose to make In-App purchases, you are using virtual money. So, it's easy for you to not think about how much these purchases are actually costing you. This is why it is important to write down in your Piggy Banker Money Journal, even when your purchases are made with virtual money.

Having to write down every time you buy an app or make an in-app purchase will help you to see that these small amounts can add up. It will also help you connect with the fact that you're using real money. You need to think about whether it makes sense to make these purchases, just like you would weigh the pros and cons about making a purchase of an item at a store. Would you rather pay $24.99 for "skins" (outfits) for your virtual character, or would you rather use that money on real clothes for yourself? You may still choose to purchase the "skins" but at least you should take the time to make that decision, as you would a real item with actual bills from your wallet.

- *Fortnite,* the popular free on-line game, has made over $1 billion in revenue from in-app purchases by players.
- 68% of surveyed *Fortnite* players said they spend money on the game. 59% of purchases were made on "skins."
- The mobile commerce categories that generate the most money are video games and accessories, toys and hobbies, and sports and fitness.
- Some kids don't realize they're spending actual money when an app asks them to pay to level up or get a better accessory for their avatar.

Money: SAVE IT

Saving for a Goal

If you have certain goals you want to save up for, you need to keep them in mind every time you spend your money on something else. You need to ask yourself if what you want to purchase today is more important or necessary to you than saving that money in order for you to be closer to having enough money to reach your goal. This goal could be a particular toy or video game; it could be a special outfit; it could be a bike, or a fishing pole – anything you want to buy yourself, but it costs enough for you to have to save up for it. You can have more than one goal on your Wish List, and they can change over time.

YOUR PIGGY BANK SAVINGS

In your Piggy Banker Money Journal, there is a column marked "Piggy Bank." Your "Piggy Bank" is like a Savings Account. In order to reach your Goals more quickly, the best thing you can do is to set aside a weekly or monthly amount for Savings in your "Piggy Bank." This is an amount that you set aside in your "SAVE" envelope, which you don't touch or consider for daily spending. You are saving this money to only spend on your Goals/Wish List Items. Having Savings will be even more important when you are older, when you need to save for a big item like a house, so it's a good idea to get in the habit of saving now. If you choose to set aside savings, you will occasionally move some money out of your spending account and add it to your "Piggy Bank" savings. Under "Money OUT", there is a line item for "Piggy Bank Deposit" – this is the amount you may choose to move out of your SPEND envelope and into your SAVE/Piggy Bank envelope to save for a Goal.

Once you use money from your Piggy Bank Savings Account on a wish list item, make sure you write in the amount next to Money OUT and subtract it from your Piggy Bank amount. If you need to use some money from your Spending Account for your wish list purchase, move that amount into your Piggy Bank first.

MONEY OUT:		
Piggy Bank Deposit	$ 10.00	→

PIGGY BANK Savings Account	
Current Piggy Bank:	$ 20.00
→ + Money IN:	+ $ 10.00
- Money OUT:	- $
New Piggy Bank:	= $ 30.00

PIGGY BANKER WISH LIST

Your wish list is a place for an item, trip, or outing that you want to save up for. You can either write down the name of what you are saving for, draw a picture of it, or paste in a picture from an advertisement or printed from the computer. You should also include the cost of the item, so you know how much you need to save up. Once you have purchased the item on your wish list goal, you can check it off and write down a new goal on the next wish list page. (Remember, if you ever decide you no longer want what's on your wish list, you can always cross it out and replace it with a new goal.)

Whenever you are going to spend any of your money, you should take a look at your wish list item and make a decision whether you really want to make that purchase or if you would rather save your money in order to be closer to reaching your wish list goal. Also, don't be too quick to drain your "bank" as soon as you have enough for your Wish List item. You should make sure you still have enough money left for items you will need to purchase in the short-term before you are able to accumulate more money. If you decided to put some of your money aside in your "SAVE/Piggy Bank" envelope to save, you can wait until that amount is enough for your wish list item, that way you will still have money in your SPEND envelope for other things. You will find your *Piggy Banker Wish List* sheets at the end of this journal.

> Don't forget to do a check-in and compare the cost of your Wish List item to how much money you currently have in your spending account or saved in your Piggy Bank. Are you getting closer?

COST:

Image: Freepik.com

Interest

Interest on money in a Savings Account can be Simple or Compound. Simple Interest is an interest percent paid just on the money you have put in the account. Compound interest is a percent paid on the money you have put in the account plus the money you have earned in interest.

SIMPLE INTEREST: Let's say the Interest Yield was 1% a year. If you have $100, the first year you would earn $100 x 1% = $1, so you would have a total of $101. The next year you would earn $100 x 1% = $1, so at the end of the second year, you would have $101 + $1 = $102.

ANNUAL COMPOUND INTEREST: With an Interest Yield of 1% a year, if you have $100, the first year you would earn $100 x 1% = $1, so you would have a total of $101. The next year you would earn 1% on $101 (instead of just on $100), so you would earn $101 x 1% = $1.01. At the end of the second year you would have $101 + $1.01 = $102.01.

Bank Account

Instead of keeping your money in a box at home, you can ask your parents about opening up a Bank Account. You can still use your Piggy Banker Money Journal to keep track of your money, but you'll need to write a check, use a debit card or withdraw money from an ATM when you want to use your money on something. Many banks offer low to no rates for students to open up an account, especially if you want to open an account at the bank your parents have an account at.

Types of Bank Accounts

CHECKING ACCOUNTS: Accounts for money you plan on spending. These accounts usually provide blank checks and a debit card for you to use. They usually don't pay you any interest or a very small amount.

SAVINGS ACCOUNTS: Accounts for money you are saving. These accounts will pay you a small amount of interest (money they pay you for keeping your money in their bank). The average savings account rate among US Banks is currently just 0.09% a year on the money you have in that account. The largest banks offer even less, around 0.01% yield a year – at that rate, a savings balance of $10,000 would earn just $1.00 a year. Though you won't earn much on it, the bank is still a safe place to keep your money.

Money: SHARE IT

Why give your money away for nothing in return? It's for the feeling you get when you know you've done something good. Ask your parents to talk to you about Charitable Giving. A study done by Indiana University, shows that parents who talk to their children throughout childhood, about charitable giving, instead of just modeling the behavior alone, significantly increases the likelihood their children will want to be charitable.

There is a line on your Piggy Banker Money Journal, labeled SHARE/Donate, for you to record money that you donate to a cause, religious organization, or individual. To make **GIVING** a habit put excess change and bills in your SHARE envelope – each time you accumulate $20 or more you can decide where you want to donate it. Any money you put into your SHARE envelope should still be part of your MONEY IN and each time you take money out of that envelope to donate it, list that under MONEY OUT on the "SHARE/Donate" line. You can also write down on that line where you donated to.

Have your parents help you make the donation in your name so that any updates on the charity get mailed or emailed directly to! you. Better yet, give your donation in person so you can see firsthand the good you are doing. Ask your parents if they want to match your donation!

There are many ways for you to be charitable with your money and your time, including:

o National Charities
o Local Charities
o Disaster Relief
o Religious Organizations
o Animal Rescue Centers
o Donate Toys for a Gift Drive
o Lemonade Stand for a Cause
o Donate Outgrown Clothes
o Do Charitable Work
o Volunteer at a Senior Center
o Help at a Soup Kitchen

Money: LOAN IT

Often, parents don't carry cash around because they are used to paying with credit cards. Sometimes, if they need cash, such as to tip the pizza delivery person, they may come to you to borrow some money. Or maybe if a sibling is short on cash and needs it in the moment, they might borrow from you. Being part of a family can sometimes mean loaning each other money every now and then, that is why there is a line item under Money OUT for "LOANS" on your Piggy Banker Money Journal. If you write down any loans you have given out, it will help you to remember to make sure that money is paid back — because sometimes people forget. This is also where you will write down any loans that you are paying back that you had received — for that write "paid back" and the person's name.

Besides giving loans, you can also get loans. Any loans your parents give you, you can put under Money IN next to the line "Other" writing next to it that it was a loan and who it was from so that you remember to pay it back. When you are older, you can get LOANS from banks to help you make big purchases like a house, car, or college education. Banks are willing to loan you money because in return, you will pay them interest on that loan.

Using Credit Cards is like getting a loan to pay for something. In the future, when you get a Credit Card from your parents to use, or eventually one of your own, it's important to pay your Credit Card balance in full each month whenever possible. This is because the interest rate the Credit Card company will charge you on any balance you haven't paid off, at the end of the month, is quite high. In fact, the average interest rate Americans pay on their credit cards is 16.5%. Credit cards should be seen as a convenience, so you don't have to carry a lot of cash around but take the risk out of it by making sure you pay off your debt every month. If you pay off your full credit card bill amount each month and not just the minimum due, you won't have to pay interest on it. Unfortunately, 45% of Americans don't pay their credit card balances in full every month and with that outstanding amount and the accumulating extra money owed due to the interest charge, it's easy to get yourself into significant debt.

Money: INVEST IT

Though you probably don't have enough money at this point in your life to INVEST it, it's still important for you to start to learn about what it means to invest your money and why it will be important for you to be comfortable with investing in the future. This section will just give you a very short overview of what a stock is and how the stock market works. You can learn more about this on our Raise Creative Investors website.

STOCK: Companies sell units (called Stock) of ownership in their company. Companies use the money they receive from the sale of stocks to do things like: create new products, hire more employees, and expand their businesses. When you buy a stock, you own a small portion of that company, so you share in the good news or bad news of how that company does. When the company does well, the price of the stock you bought can go up in price. And when the company is not doing well, the price of the stock you bought can go down. The **Stock Market** is the place where stocks are bought and sold. **Investing** in the stock market is usually meant to be for a longer time-frame because, even if stock prices go up and down, over time the stock market usually ends up higher, with the goal of selling your stock at a higher price than what you paid for it, thereby making money on your investment.

WHY INVEST? You want to invest in order to create wealth due to the power of compounding. Compounding means not only can your initial investment earn money but so can the amount it's grown to along with any interest reinvested. The Stock Market (S&P 500) has historically returned an average of 10% a year since 1926. That means starting at the age of 25, if you invest $2,000 once a year, every year, in an investment that averages a 10% annual return, it'll grow to more than $1 million after 40 years, which is right around retirement age. Investing can also help you achieve future long-term goals like buying a house one day or sending your kids to college – just like your parents may be doing for you. Currently only about 50% of all Americans invest in the Stock Market. Also, men are more likely to invest their money than women. So, the more you learn about investing now, the more likely you will be to invest in the future and build your wealth.

Weekly Money Journal Worksheet Directions

Your *Piggy Banker Money Journal* is broken down into 52 weeks of worksheets, for a total of 12 months. You can start whenever you want, whatever week it is in the year, even if it's mid-week just record for however many days are left in that week. Each week should have the same starting day, such as Sunday (start of the calendar week) or Monday (start of the school week) – just be consistent.

If there is a week where you have not brought any new money in or spent any money, then you can either record a zero for that week, or you can just not record that week and use the next worksheet when you have moved some of your money in or out. If you skip weeks, you may end up with more than 12 months of usage. There are two money journal worksheets for each week – "Breakdown of Your Expenses" and "The Piggy Banker Money Journal."

Breakdown of Your Expenses Worksheets (money you've spent):

It's important to know what you're spending your money on, that is why this sheet is broken down by item. It is then grouped by category for input into its accompanying money journal worksheet. At the end of each week, you should reflect on what you have written down on your Expenses worksheet. Are you happy with how you have spent your money and how much money you have left at the end of the week? Or will you do things differently next week – maybe not buy so much candy or cut down on your Frappuccinos.

BUDGETING – if you find yourself not having enough money for your expenses each week, you might want to start making yourself a budget. A budget is where you list out all your upcoming "Needs" and how much they cost, so that you can make sure you don't spend all your money each week on your "Wants" before making sure you have enough money to pay for your "Needs."

EXAMPLE:

Breakdown of Your Expenses WEEK:		
MONEY OUT:		
Toys/Video Games/Apps:	Lego Set	$ 21.55
	iPhone Game App	$ 1.99
		$
		$
		$
		$
TOTAL Toys/Video Games/Apps:		**$ 23.54**
Food/Beverage:	Starbucks Frappucino	$ 5.24
	Candy Bar	$ 1.50
		$
		$
		$
TOTAL Food/Beverage:		**$ 6.74**
Entertainment:	Movies	$ 14.00
		$
		$
		$
		$
		$
TOTAL Entertainment:		**$ 14.00**
Personal Items:	Jeans	$ 24.90
	iPhone Case	$ 12.50
		$
		$
		$
TOTAL Personal Items:		**$ 37.40**
For School:	Bake School	$ 2.00
		$
TOTAL School:		**$ 2.00**
For Car:	Gas	$ 20.00
		$
TOTAL Car:		**$ 20.00**
OTHER:		$
		$
		$
		$
TOTAL Other:		**$**

Breakdown of Money Journal Worksheets

1. Your Week's Starting TOTAL: At the top of the **Piggy Banker Money Journal** worksheet, write in the amount of how much money you currently have next to "Starting TOTAL" (This amount should equal all the money you have in both your SPEND and SHARE envelopes.). If you have any Money IN or Money OUT for the prior week, this Starting TOTAL will often be different each week. Also, at the very top, next to "WEEK:" you can write the starting date for that week or just a number like "Week One".

2. Current Piggy Bank: Write in the amount of money in your SAVE/Piggy Bank envelope. If this is your first week of filling out your money journal, you will need to decide if you want to start off with any of your "Starting Amount" in your Piggy Bank Savings.

3. Money IN: Write in any New Money you have brought in for each category: Allowance, Gift, Job, or Other. If this money falls into the "Other" category, write down where the money came from next to "Other." Then use a calculator to total up these categories for a "Total IN" amount.

4. Money OUT/Piggy Bank Deposit: The first line under Money OUT is for "Piggy Bank Deposit". This line is for any money you decide you want to move over to your "Savings" Piggy Bank. The best way to become a good saver is to set up a weekly, twice a month, or monthly time that you choose to move a set amount into Savings. For instance, $5 a week or $10 on the first of each month. Then you need to physically move that money from your SPEND envelope, into your SAVE/Piggy Bank envelope, and you need to record it. You can write that same amount in your "Piggy Bank" column next to "Money IN". If you've used any money from your Piggy Bank Savings, like to buy a Wish List item, put that in your Piggy Bank Column, next to "Money OUT". Then add your Piggy Bank Money IN and subtract your Piggy Bank Money Out to get your "New Piggy Bank" amount.

5. Money OUT Categories: You can take your Category Totals from your Expenses Page and input them here. The Categories are: Toys/VideoGames/Apps, Food/Beverage, Entertainment, Personal Items, For School (like for field trips or clubs), For Car (like gas if you drive), and Other. Then there is a Line Item for "SHARE/Donate," for donations, and a Line Item for "Loan", in case you loaned out any money or paid back a loan that week. Now TOTAL Up your MONEY OUT.

6. Bottom of Worksheet Calculation: At the bottom of the worksheet you will again see "Starting TOTAL", write in the amount you wrote in at the top of the page for: "Starting TOTAL." On the next two lines you will then write in your "TOTAL IN" and "TOTAL OUT" (copied from above in the worksheet). To get your "NEW TOTAL," you will take the *Starting TOTAL,* **ADD** your TOTAL IN amount and **SUBTRACT** your TOTAL OUT amount. Put this *"New TOTAL"* next to "Starting TOTAL" on your next week's journal page. Also, write in your "New Piggy Bank" savings amount for your "Current" Piggy Bank savings amount on your next journal page.

The Piggy Banker Money Journal   Week: <u>EXAMPLE</u>

Starting TOTAL: Spending Account	$ 300.00
MONEY IN:	
Allowance	$ 25.00
Gift	$ 20.00
Job	$
Other:	$
TOTAL IN:	$ 45.00
MONEY OUT:	
Piggy Bank Deposit	$ 10.00 →
Toys/Video Games/Apps	$ 23.54
Food/Beverage	$ 6.74
Entertainment	$ 14.00
Personal Items	$ 37.40
For School	$ 2.00
For Car	$ 20.00
Other	$
SHARE/Donate: Red Cross	$ 2.00
Loan to: Brother	$ 5.00
TOTAL OUT:	$ 120.68

PIGGY BANK Savings Account	
Current Piggy Bank:	$ 20.00
→+ Money IN:	+ $ 10.00
- Money OUT:	– $
= New Piggy Bank:	= $ 30.00

Starting Total	$ 300.00
+ TOTAL IN	+ $ 45.00
- TOTAL OUT	– $ 120.68
= New TOTAL put at top of next journal	= $ 224.32

Breakdown of Your Expenses WEEK:	
MONEY OUT:	
Toys/Video Games/Apps:	$
	$
	$
	$
	$
	$
TOTAL Toys/Video Games/Apps:	$
Food/Beverage:	$
	$
	$
	$
	$
TOTAL Food/Beverage:	$
Entertainment:	$
	$
	$
	$
	$
	$
TOTAL Entertainment:	$
Personal Items:	$
	$
	$
	$
	$
TOTAL Personal Items:	$
For School:	$
	$
TOTAL School:	$
For Car:	$
	$
TOTAL Car:	$
OTHER:	$
	$
	$
	$
TOTAL Other:	$

The Piggy Banker Money Journal   Week: _____

Starting TOTAL: Spending Account	$

MONEY IN:	
Allowance	$
Gift	$
Job	$
Other:	$
TOTAL IN:	$

MONEY OUT:	
Piggy Bank Deposit	$ →
Toys/Video Games/Apps	$
Food/Beverage	$
Entertainment	$
Personal Items	$
For School	$
For Car	$
Other	$
SHARE/Donate:	$
Loan to:	$
TOTAL OUT:	$

PIGGY BANK Savings Account	
Current Piggy Bank:	$
→+ Money IN:	+ $
- Money OUT:	- $
= New Piggy Bank:	= $

Starting Total	$
+ TOTAL IN	+ $
- TOTAL OUT	- $
= New TOTAL put at top of next journal	= $

Breakdown of Your Expenses WEEK:	
MONEY OUT:	
Toys/Video Games/Apps:	$
	$
	$
	$
	$
	$
TOTAL Toys/Video Games/Apps:	$
Food/Beverage:	$
	$
	$
	$
	$
TOTAL Food/Beverage:	$
Entertainment:	$
	$
	$
	$
	$
	$
TOTAL Entertainment:	$
Personal Items:	$
	$
	$
	$
	$
TOTAL Personal Items:	$
For School:	$
	$
TOTAL School:	$
For Car:	$
	$
TOTAL Car:	$
OTHER:	$
	$
	$
	$
TOTAL Other:	$

The Piggy Banker Money Journal   Week: _____

Starting TOTAL: Spending Account	$

MONEY IN:	
Allowance	$
Gift	$
Job	$
Other:	$
TOTAL IN:	$

MONEY OUT:	
Piggy Bank Deposit	$ →
Toys/Video Games/Apps	$
Food/Beverage	$
Entertainment	$
Personal Items	$
For School	$
For Car	$
Other	$
SHARE/Donate:	$
Loan to:	$
TOTAL OUT:	$

PIGGY BANK Savings Account	
Current Piggy Bank:	$
→+ Money IN:	+ $
- Money OUT:	- $
= New Piggy Bank:	= $

Starting Total	$
+ TOTAL IN	+ $
- TOTAL OUT	- $
= New TOTAL put at top of next journal	= $

Breakdown of Your Expenses WEEK:	
MONEY OUT:	
Toys/Video Games/Apps:	$
	$
	$
	$
	$
	$
TOTAL Toys/Video Games/Apps:	$
Food/Beverage:	$
	$
	$
	$
	$
TOTAL Food/Beverage:	$
Entertainment:	$
	$
	$
	$
	$
	$
TOTAL Entertainment:	$
Personal Items:	$
	$
	$
	$
	$
TOTAL Personal Items:	$
For School:	$
	$
TOTAL School:	$
For Car:	$
	$
TOTAL Car:	$
OTHER:	$
	$
	$
	$
TOTAL Other:	$

The Piggy Banker Money Journal   Week: _____

Starting TOTAL: Spending Account	$
MONEY IN:	
Allowance	$
Gift	$
Job	$
Other:	$
TOTAL IN:	$
MONEY OUT:	
Piggy Bank Deposit	$ →
Toys/Video Games/Apps	$
Food/Beverage	$
Entertainment	$
Personal Items	$
For School	$
For Car	$
Other	$
SHARE/Donate:	$
Loan to:	$
TOTAL OUT:	$

PIGGY BANK Savings Account	
Current Piggy Bank:	$
→+ Money IN:	+ $
- Money OUT:	− $
= New Piggy Bank:	**= $**

Starting Total	$
+ TOTAL IN	+ $
− TOTAL OUT	− $
= New TOTAL put at top of next journal	**= $**

Breakdown of Your Expenses WEEK:	
MONEY OUT:	
Toys/Video Games/Apps:	$
	$
	$
	$
	$
	$
TOTAL Toys/Video Games/Apps:	$
Food/Beverage:	$
	$
	$
	$
	$
TOTAL Food/Beverage:	$
Entertainment:	$
	$
	$
	$
	$
	$
TOTAL Entertainment:	$
Personal Items:	$
	$
	$
	$
	$
TOTAL Personal Items:	$
For School:	$
	$
TOTAL School:	$
For Car:	$
	$
TOTAL Car:	$
OTHER:	$
	$
	$
	$
TOTAL Other:	$

The Piggy Banker Money Journal   Week: _____

Starting TOTAL: Spending Account	$
MONEY IN:	
Allowance	$
Gift	$
Job	$
Other:	$
TOTAL IN:	$
MONEY OUT:	
Piggy Bank Deposit	$ →
Toys/Video Games/Apps	$
Food/Beverage	$
Entertainment	$
Personal Items	$
For School	$
For Car	$
Other	$
SHARE/Donate:	$
Loan to:	$
TOTAL OUT:	$

PIGGY BANK Savings Account	
Current Piggy Bank:	$
→+ Money IN:	+ $
- Money OUT:	- $
= New Piggy Bank:	= $

Starting Total	$
+ TOTAL IN	+ $
- TOTAL OUT	- $
= New TOTAL put at top of next journal	= $

Breakdown of Your Expenses WEEK:	
MONEY OUT:	
Toys/Video Games/Apps:	$
	$
	$
	$
	$
	$
TOTAL Toys/Video Games/Apps:	$
Food/Beverage:	$
	$
	$
	$
	$
TOTAL Food/Beverage:	$
Entertainment:	$
	$
	$
	$
	$
	$
TOTAL Entertainment:	$
Personal Items:	$
	$
	$
	$
	$
TOTAL Personal Items:	$
For School:	$
	$
TOTAL School:	$
For Car:	$
	$
TOTAL Car:	$
OTHER:	$
	$
	$
	$
TOTAL Other:	$

The Piggy Banker Money Journal   Week: _____

Starting TOTAL: Spending Account	$
MONEY IN:	
Allowance	$
Gift	$
Job	$
Other:	$
TOTAL IN:	$
MONEY OUT:	
Piggy Bank Deposit	$ →
Toys/Video Games/Apps	$
Food/Beverage	$
Entertainment	$
Personal Items	$
For School	$
For Car	$
Other	$
SHARE/Donate:	$
Loan to:	$
TOTAL OUT:	$

PIGGY BANK Savings Account	
Current Piggy Bank:	$
→+ Money IN:	+ $
- Money OUT:	– $
= New Piggy Bank:	= $

Starting Total	$
+ TOTAL IN	+ $
- TOTAL OUT	– $
= New TOTAL put at top of next journal	= $

Breakdown of Your Expenses WEEK:	
MONEY OUT:	
Toys/Video Games/Apps:	$
	$
	$
	$
	$
	$
TOTAL Toys/Video Games/Apps:	$
Food/Beverage:	$
	$
	$
	$
	$
TOTAL Food/Beverage:	$
Entertainment:	$
	$
	$
	$
	$
	$
TOTAL Entertainment:	$
Personal Items:	$
	$
	$
	$
	$
TOTAL Personal Items:	$
For School:	$
	$
TOTAL School:	$
For Car:	$
	$
TOTAL Car:	$
OTHER:	$
	$
	$
	$
TOTAL Other:	$

The Piggy Banker Money Journal   Week: _____

Starting TOTAL: Spending Account	$
MONEY IN:	
Allowance	$
Gift	$
Job	$
Other:	$
TOTAL IN:	$
MONEY OUT:	
Piggy Bank Deposit	$ →
Toys/Video Games/Apps	$
Food/Beverage	$
Entertainment	$
Personal Items	$
For School	$
For Car	$
Other	$
SHARE/Donate:	$
Loan to:	$
TOTAL OUT:	$

PIGGY BANK Savings Account	
Current Piggy Bank:	$
→+ Money IN:	+ $
– Money OUT:	– $
= New Piggy Bank:	= $

Starting Total	$
+ TOTAL IN	+ $
– TOTAL OUT	– $
= New TOTAL put at top of next journal	= $

Breakdown of Your Expenses WEEK:	
MONEY OUT:	
Toys/Video Games/Apps:	$
	$
	$
	$
	$
	$
TOTAL Toys/Video Games/Apps:	$
Food/Beverage:	$
	$
	$
	$
	$
TOTAL Food/Beverage:	$
Entertainment:	$
	$
	$
	$
	$
	$
TOTAL Entertainment:	$
Personal Items:	$
	$
	$
	$
	$
TOTAL Personal Items:	$
For School:	$
	$
TOTAL School:	$
For Car:	$
	$
TOTAL Car:	$
OTHER:	$
	$
	$
	$
TOTAL Other:	$

The Piggy Banker Money Journal   Week: _____

Starting TOTAL: Spending Account	$
MONEY IN:	
Allowance	$
Gift	$
Job	$
Other:	$
TOTAL IN:	$
MONEY OUT:	
Piggy Bank Deposit	$ →
Toys/Video Games/Apps	$
Food/Beverage	$
Entertainment	$
Personal Items	$
For School	$
For Car	$
Other	$
SHARE/Donate:	$
Loan to:	$
TOTAL OUT:	$

PIGGY BANK Savings Account	
Current Piggy Bank:	$
→+ Money IN:	+ $
- Money OUT:	- $
= New Piggy Bank:	= $

Starting Total	$
+ TOTAL IN	+ $
- TOTAL OUT	- $
= New TOTAL put at top of next journal	= $

Breakdown of Your Expenses WEEK:	
MONEY OUT:	
Toys/Video Games/Apps:	$
	$
	$
	$
	$
	$
TOTAL Toys/Video Games/Apps:	$
Food/Beverage:	$
	$
	$
	$
	$
TOTAL Food/Beverage:	$
Entertainment:	$
	$
	$
	$
	$
	$
TOTAL Entertainment:	$
Personal Items:	$
	$
	$
	$
	$
TOTAL Personal Items:	$
For School:	$
	$
TOTAL School:	$
For Car:	$
	$
TOTAL Car:	$
OTHER:	$
	$
	$
	$
TOTAL Other:	$

The Piggy Banker Money Journal   Week: _____

Starting TOTAL: Spending Account	$		PIGGY BANK Savings Account	
MONEY IN:			Current Piggy Bank:	$
Allowance	$			
Gift	$			
Job	$			
Other:	$			
TOTAL IN:	$			
MONEY OUT:				
Piggy Bank Deposit	$ →		→+ Money IN:	+ $
Toys/Video Games/Apps	$			
Food/Beverage	$		− Money OUT:	− $
Entertainment	$			
Personal Items	$			
For School	$			
For Car	$			
Other	$			
SHARE/Donate:	$			
Loan to:	$		= New Piggy Bank:	= $
TOTAL OUT:	$			

Starting Total	$
+ TOTAL IN	+ $
− TOTAL OUT	− $
= New TOTAL put at top of next journal	= $

Breakdown of Your Expenses WEEK:	
MONEY OUT:	
Toys/Video Games/Apps:	$
	$
	$
	$
	$
	$
TOTAL Toys/Video Games/Apps:	$
Food/Beverage:	$
	$
	$
	$
	$
TOTAL Food/Beverage:	$
Entertainment:	$
	$
	$
	$
	$
	$
TOTAL Entertainment:	$
Personal Items:	$
	$
	$
	$
	$
TOTAL Personal Items:	$
For School:	$
	$
TOTAL School:	$
For Car:	$
	$
TOTAL Car:	$
OTHER:	$
	$
	$
	$
TOTAL Other:	$

The Piggy Banker Money Journal   Week: _____

Starting TOTAL: Spending Account	$
MONEY IN:	
Allowance	$
Gift	$
Job	$
Other:	$
TOTAL IN:	$
MONEY OUT:	
Piggy Bank Deposit	$ →
Toys/Video Games/Apps	$
Food/Beverage	$
Entertainment	$
Personal Items	$
For School	$
For Car	$
Other	$
SHARE/Donate:	$
Loan to:	$
TOTAL OUT:	$

PIGGY BANK Savings Account	
Current Piggy Bank:	$
→ + Money IN:	+ $
− Money OUT:	− $
= New Piggy Bank:	= $

Starting Total	$
+ TOTAL IN	+ $
− TOTAL OUT	− $
= New TOTAL put at top of next journal	= $

Breakdown of Your Expenses WEEK:	
MONEY OUT:	
Toys/Video Games/Apps:	$
	$
	$
	$
	$
	$
TOTAL Toys/Video Games/Apps:	$
Food/Beverage:	$
	$
	$
	$
	$
TOTAL Food/Beverage:	$
Entertainment:	$
	$
	$
	$
	$
	$
TOTAL Entertainment:	$
Personal Items:	$
	$
	$
	$
	$
TOTAL Personal Items:	$
For School:	$
	$
TOTAL School:	$
For Car:	$
	$
TOTAL Car:	$
OTHER:	$
	$
	$
	$
TOTAL Other:	$

The Piggy Banker Money Journal   Week: _____

Starting TOTAL: Spending Account	$
MONEY IN:	
Allowance	$
Gift	$
Job	$
Other:	$
TOTAL IN:	$
MONEY OUT:	
Piggy Bank Deposit	$ →
Toys/Video Games/Apps	$
Food/Beverage	$
Entertainment	$
Personal Items	$
For School	$
For Car	$
Other	$
SHARE/Donate:	$
Loan to:	$
TOTAL OUT:	$

PIGGY BANK Savings Account	
Current Piggy Bank:	$
→+ Money IN:	+ $
- Money OUT:	_ $
= New Piggy Bank:	**= $**

Starting Total	$
+ TOTAL IN	+ $
- TOTAL OUT	- $
= New TOTAL put at top of next journal	= $

Breakdown of Your Expenses WEEK:	
MONEY OUT:	
Toys/Video Games/Apps:	$
	$
	$
	$
	$
	$
TOTAL Toys/Video Games/Apps:	$
Food/Beverage:	$
	$
	$
	$
	$
TOTAL Food/Beverage:	$
Entertainment:	$
	$
	$
	$
	$
	$
TOTAL Entertainment:	$
Personal Items:	$
	$
	$
	$
	$
TOTAL Personal Items:	$
For School:	$
	$
TOTAL School:	$
For Car:	$
	$
TOTAL Car:	$
OTHER:	$
	$
	$
	$
TOTAL Other:	$

The Piggy Banker Money Journal   Week: _____

Starting TOTAL: Spending Account	$

MONEY IN:	
Allowance	$
Gift	$
Job	$
Other:	$
TOTAL IN:	$

MONEY OUT:		
Piggy Bank Deposit	$	→
Toys/Video Games/Apps	$	
Food/Beverage	$	
Entertainment	$	
Personal Items	$	
For School	$	
For Car	$	
Other	$	
SHARE/Donate:	$	
Loan to:	$	
TOTAL OUT:	$	

PIGGY BANK Savings Account	
Current Piggy Bank:	$
→+ Money IN:	+ $
- Money OUT:	- $
= New Piggy Bank:	= $

Starting Total	$
+ TOTAL IN	+ $
- TOTAL OUT	- $
= New TOTAL put at top of next journal	= $

Breakdown of Your Expenses WEEK:	
MONEY OUT:	
Toys/Video Games/Apps:	$
	$
	$
	$
	$
	$
TOTAL Toys/Video Games/Apps:	$
Food/Beverage:	$
	$
	$
	$
	$
TOTAL Food/Beverage:	$
Entertainment:	$
	$
	$
	$
	$
	$
TOTAL Entertainment:	$
Personal Items:	$
	$
	$
	$
	$
TOTAL Personal Items:	$
For School:	$
	$
TOTAL School:	$
For Car:	$
	$
TOTAL Car:	$
OTHER:	$
	$
	$
	$
TOTAL Other:	$

The Piggy Banker Money Journal

Week: _____

Starting TOTAL: Spending Account	$
MONEY IN:	
Allowance	$
Gift	$
Job	$
Other:	$
TOTAL IN:	$
MONEY OUT:	
Piggy Bank Deposit	$ →
Toys/Video Games/Apps	$
Food/Beverage	$
Entertainment	$
Personal Items	$
For School	$
For Car	$
Other	$
SHARE/Donate:	$
Loan to:	$
TOTAL OUT:	$

PIGGY BANK Savings Account	
Current Piggy Bank:	$
→+ Money IN:	+ $
- Money OUT:	- $
= New Piggy Bank:	= $

Starting Total	$
+ TOTAL IN	+ $
- TOTAL OUT	- $
= New TOTAL put at top of next journal	= $

Breakdown of Your Expenses WEEK:	
MONEY OUT:	
Toys/Video Games/Apps:	$
	$
	$
	$
	$
	$
TOTAL Toys/Video Games/Apps:	$
Food/Beverage:	$
	$
	$
	$
	$
TOTAL Food/Beverage:	$
Entertainment:	$
	$
	$
	$
	$
	$
TOTAL Entertainment:	$
Personal Items:	$
	$
	$
	$
	$
TOTAL Personal Items:	$
For School:	$
	$
TOTAL School:	$
For Car:	$
	$
TOTAL Car:	$
OTHER:	$
	$
	$
	$
TOTAL Other:	$

The Piggy Banker Money Journal   Week: _____

Starting TOTAL: Spending Account	$
MONEY IN:	
Allowance	$
Gift	$
Job	$
Other:	$
TOTAL IN:	$
MONEY OUT:	
Piggy Bank Deposit	$ →
Toys/Video Games/Apps	$
Food/Beverage	$
Entertainment	$
Personal Items	$
For School	$
For Car	$
Other	$
SHARE/Donate:	$
Loan to:	$
TOTAL OUT:	$

PIGGY BANK Savings Account	
Current Piggy Bank:	$
→+ Money IN:	+ $
- Money OUT:	- $
= New Piggy Bank:	= $

Starting Total	$
+ TOTAL IN	+ $
- TOTAL OUT	- $
= New TOTAL put at top of next journal	= $

Breakdown of Your Expenses WEEK:	
MONEY OUT:	
Toys/Video Games/Apps:	$
	$
	$
	$
	$
	$
TOTAL Toys/Video Games/Apps:	$
Food/Beverage:	$
	$
	$
	$
	$
TOTAL Food/Beverage:	$
Entertainment:	$
	$
	$
	$
	$
	$
TOTAL Entertainment:	$
Personal Items:	$
	$
	$
	$
	$
TOTAL Personal Items:	$
For School:	$
	$
TOTAL School:	$
For Car:	$
	$
TOTAL Car:	$
OTHER:	$
	$
	$
	$
	$
TOTAL Other:	$

The Piggy Banker Money Journal   Week: _____

Starting TOTAL: Spending Account	$
MONEY IN:	
Allowance	$
Gift	$
Job	$
Other:	$
TOTAL IN:	$
MONEY OUT:	
Piggy Bank Deposit	$ →
Toys/Video Games/Apps	$
Food/Beverage	$
Entertainment	$
Personal Items	$
For School	$
For Car	$
Other	$
SHARE/Donate:	$
Loan to:	$
TOTAL OUT:	$

PIGGY BANK Savings Account	
Current Piggy Bank:	$
→+ Money IN:	+ $
- Money OUT:	_ $
= New Piggy Bank:	= $

Starting Total	$
+ TOTAL IN	+ $
- TOTAL OUT	- $
= New TOTAL put at top of next journal	= $

Breakdown of Your Expenses WEEK:	
MONEY OUT:	
Toys/Video Games/Apps:	$
	$
	$
	$
	$
	$
TOTAL Toys/Video Games/Apps:	$
Food/Beverage:	$
	$
	$
	$
	$
TOTAL Food/Beverage:	$
Entertainment:	$
	$
	$
	$
	$
	$
TOTAL Entertainment:	$
Personal Items:	$
	$
	$
	$
	$
TOTAL Personal Items:	$
For School:	$
	$
TOTAL School:	$
For Car:	$
	$
TOTAL Car:	$
OTHER:	$
	$
	$
	$
TOTAL Other:	$

The Piggy Banker Money Journal   Week: _____

Starting TOTAL: Spending Account	$

MONEY IN:	
Allowance	$
Gift	$
Job	$
Other:	$
TOTAL IN:	$

MONEY OUT:		
Piggy Bank Deposit	$	→
Toys/Video Games/Apps	$	
Food/Beverage	$	
Entertainment	$	
Personal Items	$	
For School	$	
For Car	$	
Other	$	
SHARE/Donate:	$	
Loan to:	$	
TOTAL OUT:	$	

PIGGY BANK Savings Account	
Current Piggy Bank:	$
→+ Money IN:	+ $
- Money OUT:	- $
= New Piggy Bank:	= $

Starting Total	$
+ TOTAL IN	+ $
- TOTAL OUT	- $
= New TOTAL put at top of next journal	= $

Breakdown of Your Expenses WEEK:	
MONEY OUT:	
Toys/Video Games/Apps:	$
	$
	$
	$
	$
	$
TOTAL Toys/Video Games/Apps:	$
Food/Beverage:	$
	$
	$
	$
	$
TOTAL Food/Beverage:	$
Entertainment:	$
	$
	$
	$
	$
	$
TOTAL Entertainment:	$
Personal Items:	$
	$
	$
	$
	$
TOTAL Personal Items:	$
For School:	$
	$
TOTAL School:	$
For Car:	$
	$
TOTAL Car:	$
OTHER:	$
	$
	$
	$
TOTAL Other:	$

The Piggy Banker Money Journal

Week: _____

Starting TOTAL: Spending Account	$
MONEY IN:	
Allowance	$
Gift	$
Job	$
Other:	$
TOTAL IN:	$
MONEY OUT:	
Piggy Bank Deposit	$ →
Toys/Video Games/Apps	$
Food/Beverage	$
Entertainment	$
Personal Items	$
For School	$
For Car	$
Other	$
SHARE/Donate:	$
Loan to:	$
TOTAL OUT:	$

PIGGY BANK Savings Account	
Current Piggy Bank:	$
→ + Money IN:	+ $
- Money OUT:	− $
= New Piggy Bank:	= $

Starting Total	$
+ TOTAL IN	+ $
- TOTAL OUT	− $
= New TOTAL put at top of next journal	= $

Breakdown of Your Expenses WEEK:	
MONEY OUT:	
Toys/Video Games/Apps:	$
	$
	$
	$
	$
	$
TOTAL Toys/Video Games/Apps:	$
Food/Beverage:	$
	$
	$
	$
	$
TOTAL Food/Beverage:	$
Entertainment:	$
	$
	$
	$
	$
	$
TOTAL Entertainment:	$
Personal Items:	$
	$
	$
	$
	$
TOTAL Personal Items:	$
For School:	$
	$
TOTAL School:	$
For Car:	$
	$
TOTAL Car:	$
OTHER:	$
	$
	$
	$
TOTAL Other:	$

The Piggy Banker Money Journal   Week: _____

Starting TOTAL: Spending Account	$

MONEY IN:	
Allowance	$
Gift	$
Job	$
Other:	$
TOTAL IN:	$

MONEY OUT:	
Piggy Bank Deposit	$ →
Toys/Video Games/Apps	$
Food/Beverage	$
Entertainment	$
Personal Items	$
For School	$
For Car	$
Other	$
SHARE/Donate:	$
Loan to:	$
TOTAL OUT:	$

PIGGY BANK Savings Account	
Current Piggy Bank:	$
→+ Money IN:	+ $
– Money OUT:	– $
= New Piggy Bank:	= $

Starting Total	$
+ TOTAL IN	+ $
– TOTAL OUT	– $
= New TOTAL put at top of next journal	= $

Breakdown of Your Expenses WEEK:	
MONEY OUT:	
Toys/Video Games/Apps:	$
	$
	$
	$
	$
	$
TOTAL Toys/Video Games/Apps:	$
Food/Beverage:	$
	$
	$
	$
	$
TOTAL Food/Beverage:	$
Entertainment:	$
	$
	$
	$
	$
	$
TOTAL Entertainment:	$
Personal Items:	$
	$
	$
	$
	$
TOTAL Personal Items:	$
For School:	$
	$
TOTAL School:	$
For Car:	$
	$
TOTAL Car:	$
OTHER:	$
	$
	$
	$
TOTAL Other:	$

The Piggy Banker Money Journal   Week: _____

Starting TOTAL: Spending Account	$
MONEY IN:	
Allowance	$
Gift	$
Job	$
Other:	$
TOTAL IN:	$
MONEY OUT:	
Piggy Bank Deposit	$ →
Toys/Video Games/Apps	$
Food/Beverage	$
Entertainment	$
Personal Items	$
For School	$
For Car	$
Other	$
SHARE/Donate:	$
Loan to:	$
TOTAL OUT:	$

PIGGY BANK Savings Account	
Current Piggy Bank:	$
→+ Money IN:	+ $
- Money OUT:	_ $
= New Piggy Bank:	**= $**

Starting Total	$
+ TOTAL IN	+ $
- TOTAL OUT	- $
= New TOTAL put at top of next journal	= $

Breakdown of Your Expenses WEEK:	
MONEY OUT:	
Toys/Video Games/Apps:	$
	$
	$
	$
	$
	$
TOTAL Toys/Video Games/Apps:	$
Food/Beverage:	$
	$
	$
	$
	$
TOTAL Food/Beverage:	$
Entertainment:	$
	$
	$
	$
	$
	$
TOTAL Entertainment:	$
Personal Items:	$
	$
	$
	$
	$
TOTAL Personal Items:	$
For School:	$
	$
TOTAL School:	$
For Car:	$
	$
TOTAL Car:	$
OTHER:	$
	$
	$
	$
TOTAL Other:	$

The Piggy Banker Money Journal   Week: _____

Starting TOTAL: Spending Account	$
MONEY IN:	
Allowance	$
Gift	$
Job	$
Other:	$
TOTAL IN:	$
MONEY OUT:	
Piggy Bank Deposit	$ →
Toys/Video Games/Apps	$
Food/Beverage	$
Entertainment	$
Personal Items	$
For School	$
For Car	$
Other	$
SHARE/Donate:	$
Loan to:	$
TOTAL OUT:	$

PIGGY BANK Savings Account	
Current Piggy Bank:	$
→+ Money IN:	+ $
- Money OUT:	– $
= New Piggy Bank:	= $

Starting Total	$
+ TOTAL IN	+ $
- TOTAL OUT	– $
= New TOTAL put at top of next journal	= $

Breakdown of Your Expenses WEEK:	
MONEY OUT:	
Toys/Video Games/Apps:	$
	$
	$
	$
	$
	$
TOTAL Toys/Video Games/Apps:	$
Food/Beverage:	$
	$
	$
	$
	$
TOTAL Food/Beverage:	$
Entertainment:	$
	$
	$
	$
	$
	$
TOTAL Entertainment:	$
Personal Items:	$
	$
	$
	$
	$
TOTAL Personal Items:	$
For School:	$
	$
TOTAL School:	$
For Car:	$
	$
TOTAL Car:	$
OTHER:	$
	$
	$
	$
TOTAL Other:	$

The Piggy Banker Money Journal   Week: _____

Starting TOTAL: Spending Account	$
MONEY IN:	
Allowance	$
Gift	$
Job	$
Other:	$
TOTAL IN:	$
MONEY OUT:	
Piggy Bank Deposit	$ →
Toys/Video Games/Apps	$
Food/Beverage	$
Entertainment	$
Personal Items	$
For School	$
For Car	$
Other	$
SHARE/Donate:	$
Loan to:	$
TOTAL OUT:	$

PIGGY BANK Savings Account	
Current Piggy Bank:	$
→+ Money IN:	+ $
- Money OUT:	_ $
= New Piggy Bank:	= $

Starting Total	$
+ TOTAL IN	+ $
- TOTAL OUT	- $
= New TOTAL put at top of next journal	= $

Breakdown of Your Expenses WEEK:	
MONEY OUT:	
Toys/Video Games/Apps:	$
	$
	$
	$
	$
	$
TOTAL Toys/Video Games/Apps:	$
Food/Beverage:	$
	$
	$
	$
	$
TOTAL Food/Beverage:	$
Entertainment:	$
	$
	$
	$
	$
	$
TOTAL Entertainment:	$
Personal Items:	$
	$
	$
	$
	$
TOTAL Personal Items:	$
For School:	$
	$
TOTAL School:	$
For Car:	$
	$
TOTAL Car:	$
OTHER:	$
	$
	$
	$
TOTAL Other:	$

The Piggy Banker Money Journal   Week: _____

Starting TOTAL: Spending Account	$
MONEY IN:	
Allowance	$
Gift	$
Job	$
Other:	$
TOTAL IN:	$
MONEY OUT:	
Piggy Bank Deposit	$ →
Toys/Video Games/Apps	$
Food/Beverage	$
Entertainment	$
Personal Items	$
For School	$
For Car	$
Other	$
SHARE/Donate:	$
Loan to:	$
TOTAL OUT:	$

PIGGY BANK Savings Account	
Current Piggy Bank:	$
→+ Money IN:	+ $
- Money OUT:	_ $
= New Piggy Bank:	= $

Starting Total	$
+ TOTAL IN	+ $
- TOTAL OUT	- $
= New TOTAL put at top of next journal	= $

Breakdown of Your Expenses WEEK:	
MONEY OUT:	
Toys/Video Games/Apps:	$
	$
	$
	$
	$
	$
TOTAL Toys/Video Games/Apps:	$
Food/Beverage:	$
	$
	$
	$
	$
TOTAL Food/Beverage:	$
Entertainment:	$
	$
	$
	$
	$
	$
TOTAL Entertainment:	$
Personal Items:	$
	$
	$
	$
	$
TOTAL Personal Items:	$
For School:	$
	$
TOTAL School:	$
For Car:	$
	$
TOTAL Car:	$
OTHER:	$
	$
	$
	$
TOTAL Other:	$

The Piggy Banker Money Journal   Week: _____

Starting TOTAL: Spending Account	$
MONEY IN:	
Allowance	$
Gift	$
Job	$
Other:	$
TOTAL IN:	$
MONEY OUT:	
Piggy Bank Deposit	$ →
Toys/Video Games/Apps	$
Food/Beverage	$
Entertainment	$
Personal Items	$
For School	$
For Car	$
Other	$
SHARE/Donate:	$
Loan to:	$
TOTAL OUT:	$

PIGGY BANK Savings Account	
Current Piggy Bank:	$
→ + Money IN:	+ $
- Money OUT:	– $
= New Piggy Bank:	= $

Starting Total	$
+ TOTAL IN	+ $
– TOTAL OUT	– $
= New TOTAL put at top of next journal	= $

Breakdown of Your Expenses WEEK:	
MONEY OUT:	
Toys/Video Games/Apps:	$
	$
	$
	$
	$
	$
TOTAL Toys/Video Games/Apps:	$
Food/Beverage:	$
	$
	$
	$
	$
TOTAL Food/Beverage:	$
Entertainment:	$
	$
	$
	$
	$
	$
TOTAL Entertainment:	$
Personal Items:	$
	$
	$
	$
	$
TOTAL Personal Items:	$
For School:	$
	$
TOTAL School:	$
For Car:	$
	$
TOTAL Car:	$
OTHER:	$
	$
	$
	$
TOTAL Other:	$

The Piggy Banker Money Journal   Week: _____

Starting TOTAL: Spending Account	$
MONEY IN:	
Allowance	$
Gift	$
Job	$
Other:	$
TOTAL IN:	$
MONEY OUT:	
Piggy Bank Deposit	$ →
Toys/Video Games/Apps	$
Food/Beverage	$
Entertainment	$
Personal Items	$
For School	$
For Car	$
Other	$
SHARE/Donate:	$
Loan to:	$
TOTAL OUT:	$

PIGGY BANK Savings Account	
Current Piggy Bank:	$
→+ Money IN:	+ $
- Money OUT:	- $
= New Piggy Bank:	= $

Starting Total	$
+ TOTAL IN	+ $
- TOTAL OUT	- $
= New TOTAL put at top of next journal	= $

Breakdown of Your Expenses WEEK:	
MONEY OUT:	
Toys/Video Games/Apps:	$
	$
	$
	$
	$
	$
TOTAL Toys/Video Games/Apps:	$
Food/Beverage:	$
	$
	$
	$
	$
TOTAL Food/Beverage:	$
Entertainment:	$
	$
	$
	$
	$
	$
TOTAL Entertainment:	$
Personal Items:	$
	$
	$
	$
	$
TOTAL Personal Items:	$
For School:	$
	$
TOTAL School:	$
For Car:	$
	$
TOTAL Car:	$
OTHER:	$
	$
	$
	$
TOTAL Other:	$

The Piggy Banker Money Journal   Week: _____

Starting TOTAL: Spending Account	$

MONEY IN:	
Allowance	$
Gift	$
Job	$
Other:	$
TOTAL IN:	$

MONEY OUT:	
Piggy Bank Deposit	$ →
Toys/Video Games/Apps	$
Food/Beverage	$
Entertainment	$
Personal Items	$
For School	$
For Car	$
Other	$
SHARE/Donate:	$
Loan to:	$
TOTAL OUT:	$

PIGGY BANK Savings Account	
Current Piggy Bank:	$
→+ Money IN:	+ $
- Money OUT:	- $
= New Piggy Bank:	= $

Starting Total	$
+ TOTAL IN	+ $
- TOTAL OUT	- $
= New TOTAL put at top of next journal	= $

Breakdown of Your Expenses WEEK:	
MONEY OUT:	
Toys/Video Games/Apps:	$
	$
	$
	$
	$
	$
TOTAL Toys/Video Games/Apps:	$
Food/Beverage:	$
	$
	$
	$
	$
TOTAL Food/Beverage:	$
Entertainment:	$
	$
	$
	$
	$
	$
TOTAL Entertainment:	$
Personal Items:	$
	$
	$
	$
	$
TOTAL Personal Items:	$
For School:	$
	$
TOTAL School:	$
For Car:	$
	$
TOTAL Car:	$
OTHER:	$
	$
	$
	$
TOTAL Other:	$

The Piggy Banker Money Journal   Week: _____

Starting TOTAL: Spending Account	$
MONEY IN:	
Allowance	$
Gift	$
Job	$
Other:	$
TOTAL IN:	$
MONEY OUT:	
Piggy Bank Deposit	$ →
Toys/Video Games/Apps	$
Food/Beverage	$
Entertainment	$
Personal Items	$
For School	$
For Car	$
Other	$
SHARE/Donate:	$
Loan to:	$
TOTAL OUT:	$

PIGGY BANK Savings Account	
Current Piggy Bank:	$
→+ Money IN:	+ $
− Money OUT:	− $
= New **Piggy Bank:**	= $

Starting Total	$
+ TOTAL IN	+ $
− TOTAL OUT	− $
= New TOTAL put at top of next journal	= $

Breakdown of Your Expenses WEEK:	
MONEY OUT:	
Toys/Video Games/Apps:	$
	$
	$
	$
	$
	$
TOTAL Toys/Video Games/Apps:	$
Food/Beverage:	$
	$
	$
	$
	$
TOTAL Food/Beverage:	$
Entertainment:	$
	$
	$
	$
	$
	$
TOTAL Entertainment:	$
Personal Items:	$
	$
	$
	$
	$
TOTAL Personal Items:	$
For School:	$
	$
TOTAL School:	$
For Car:	$
	$
TOTAL Car:	$
OTHER:	$
	$
	$
	$
TOTAL Other:	$

The Piggy Banker Money Journal   Week: _____

Starting TOTAL: Spending Account	$
MONEY IN:	
Allowance	$
Gift	$
Job	$
Other:	$
TOTAL IN:	$
MONEY OUT:	
Piggy Bank Deposit	$ →
Toys/Video Games/Apps	$
Food/Beverage	$
Entertainment	$
Personal Items	$
For School	$
For Car	$
Other	$
SHARE/Donate:	$
Loan to:	$
TOTAL OUT:	$

PIGGY BANK Savings Account	
Current Piggy Bank:	$
→+ Money IN:	+ $
- Money OUT:	_ $
= New Piggy Bank:	= $

Starting Total	$
+ TOTAL IN	+ $
- TOTAL OUT	- $
= New TOTAL put at top of next journal	= $

Breakdown of Your Expenses WEEK:	
MONEY OUT:	
Toys/Video Games/Apps:	$
	$
	$
	$
	$
	$
TOTAL Toys/Video Games/Apps:	$
Food/Beverage:	$
	$
	$
	$
	$
TOTAL Food/Beverage:	$
Entertainment:	$
	$
	$
	$
	$
	$
TOTAL Entertainment:	$
Personal Items:	$
	$
	$
	$
	$
TOTAL Personal Items:	$
For School:	$
	$
TOTAL School:	$
For Car:	$
	$
TOTAL Car:	$
OTHER:	$
	$
	$
	$
TOTAL Other:	$

The Piggy Banker Money Journal   Week: _____

Starting TOTAL: Spending Account	$
MONEY IN:	
Allowance	$
Gift	$
Job	$
Other:	$
TOTAL IN:	$
MONEY OUT:	
Piggy Bank Deposit	$ →
Toys/Video Games/Apps	$
Food/Beverage	$
Entertainment	$
Personal Items	$
For School	$
For Car	$
Other	$
SHARE/Donate:	$
Loan to:	$
TOTAL OUT:	$

PIGGY BANK Savings Account	
Current Piggy Bank:	$
→+ Money IN:	+ $
− Money OUT:	− $
= New Piggy Bank:	= $

Starting Total	$
+ TOTAL IN	+ $
− TOTAL OUT	− $
= New TOTAL put at top of next journal	= $

Breakdown of Your Expenses WEEK:	
MONEY OUT:	
Toys/Video Games/Apps:	$
	$
	$
	$
	$
	$
TOTAL Toys/Video Games/Apps:	$
Food/Beverage:	$
	$
	$
	$
	$
TOTAL Food/Beverage:	$
Entertainment:	$
	$
	$
	$
	$
	$
TOTAL Entertainment:	$
Personal Items:	$
	$
	$
	$
	$
TOTAL Personal Items:	$
For School:	$
	$
TOTAL School:	$
For Car:	$
	$
TOTAL Car:	$
OTHER:	$
	$
	$
	$
TOTAL Other:	$

The Piggy Banker Money Journal   Week: _____

Starting TOTAL: Spending Account	$
MONEY IN:	
Allowance	$
Gift	$
Job	$
Other:	$
TOTAL IN:	$
MONEY OUT:	
Piggy Bank Deposit	$ →
Toys/Video Games/Apps	$
Food/Beverage	$
Entertainment	$
Personal Items	$
For School	$
For Car	$
Other	$
SHARE/Donate:	$
Loan to:	$
TOTAL OUT:	$

PIGGY BANK Savings Account	
Current Piggy Bank:	$
→+ Money IN:	+ $
- Money OUT:	_ $
= New Piggy Bank:	= $

Starting Total	$
+ TOTAL IN	+ $
- TOTAL OUT	- $
= New TOTAL put at top of next journal	= $

Breakdown of Your Expenses WEEK:	
MONEY OUT:	
Toys/Video Games/Apps:	$
	$
	$
	$
	$
	$
TOTAL Toys/Video Games/Apps:	$
Food/Beverage:	$
	$
	$
	$
	$
TOTAL Food/Beverage:	$
Entertainment:	$
	$
	$
	$
	$
	$
TOTAL Entertainment:	$
Personal Items:	$
	$
	$
	$
	$
TOTAL Personal Items:	$
For School:	$
	$
TOTAL School:	$
For Car:	$
	$
TOTAL Car:	$
OTHER:	$
	$
	$
	$
TOTAL Other:	$

The Piggy Banker Money Journal   Week: _____

Starting TOTAL: Spending Account	$
MONEY IN:	
Allowance	$
Gift	$
Job	$
Other:	$
TOTAL IN:	$
MONEY OUT:	
Piggy Bank Deposit	$ →
Toys/Video Games/Apps	$
Food/Beverage	$
Entertainment	$
Personal Items	$
For School	$
For Car	$
Other	$
SHARE/Donate:	$
Loan to:	$
TOTAL OUT:	$

PIGGY BANK Savings Account	
Current Piggy Bank:	$
→+ Money IN:	+ $
- Money OUT:	- $
= New Piggy Bank:	**= $**

Starting Total	$
+ TOTAL IN	+ $
- TOTAL OUT	- $
= New TOTAL put at top of next journal	= $

Breakdown of Your Expenses WEEK:	
MONEY OUT:	
Toys/Video Games/Apps:	$
	$
	$
	$
	$
	$
TOTAL Toys/Video Games/Apps:	$
Food/Beverage:	$
	$
	$
	$
	$
TOTAL Food/Beverage:	$
Entertainment:	$
	$
	$
	$
	$
	$
TOTAL Entertainment:	$
Personal Items:	$
	$
	$
	$
	$
TOTAL Personal Items:	$
For School:	$
	$
TOTAL School:	$
For Car:	$
	$
TOTAL Car:	$
OTHER:	$
	$
	$
	$
TOTAL Other:	$

The Piggy Banker Money Journal   Week: _____

Starting TOTAL: Spending Account	$
MONEY IN:	
Allowance	$
Gift	$
Job	$
Other:	$
TOTAL IN:	$
MONEY OUT:	
Piggy Bank Deposit	$ →
Toys/Video Games/Apps	$
Food/Beverage	$
Entertainment	$
Personal Items	$
For School	$
For Car	$
Other	$
SHARE/Donate:	$
Loan to:	$
TOTAL OUT:	$

PIGGY BANK Savings Account	
Current Piggy Bank:	$
→+ Money IN:	+ $
– Money OUT:	– $
= New Piggy Bank:	**= $**

Starting Total	$
+ TOTAL IN	+ $
– TOTAL OUT	– $
= New TOTAL put at top of next journal	**= $**

Breakdown of Your Expenses WEEK:	
MONEY OUT:	
Toys/Video Games/Apps:	$
	$
	$
	$
	$
	$
TOTAL Toys/Video Games/Apps:	$
Food/Beverage:	$
	$
	$
	$
	$
TOTAL Food/Beverage:	$
Entertainment:	$
	$
	$
	$
	$
	$
TOTAL Entertainment:	$
Personal Items:	$
	$
	$
	$
	$
TOTAL Personal Items:	$
For School:	$
	$
TOTAL School:	$
For Car:	$
	$
TOTAL Car:	$
OTHER:	$
	$
	$
	$
TOTAL Other:	$

The Piggy Banker Money Journal   Week: _____

Starting TOTAL: Spending Account	$
MONEY IN:	
Allowance	$
Gift	$
Job	$
Other:	$
TOTAL IN:	$
MONEY OUT:	
Piggy Bank Deposit	$ →
Toys/Video Games/Apps	$
Food/Beverage	$
Entertainment	$
Personal Items	$
For School	$
For Car	$
Other	$
SHARE/Donate:	$
Loan to:	$
TOTAL OUT:	$

PIGGY BANK Savings Account	
Current Piggy Bank:	$
→+ Money IN:	+ $
- Money OUT:	- $
= New Piggy Bank:	= $

Starting Total	$
+ TOTAL IN	+ $
- TOTAL OUT	- $
= New TOTAL put at top of next journal	= $

Breakdown of Your Expenses WEEK:	
MONEY OUT:	
Toys/Video Games/Apps:	$
	$
	$
	$
	$
	$
TOTAL Toys/Video Games/Apps:	$
Food/Beverage:	$
	$
	$
	$
	$
TOTAL Food/Beverage:	$
Entertainment:	$
	$
	$
	$
	$
	$
TOTAL Entertainment:	$
Personal Items:	$
	$
	$
	$
	$
TOTAL Personal Items:	$
For School:	$
	$
TOTAL School:	$
For Car:	$
	$
TOTAL Car:	$
OTHER:	$
	$
	$
	$
TOTAL Other:	$

The Piggy Banker Money Journal   Week: _____

Starting TOTAL: Spending Account	$

MONEY IN:	
Allowance	$
Gift	$
Job	$
Other:	$
TOTAL IN:	$

MONEY OUT:		
Piggy Bank Deposit	$	→
Toys/Video Games/Apps	$	
Food/Beverage	$	
Entertainment	$	
Personal Items	$	
For School	$	
For Car	$	
Other	$	
SHARE/Donate:	$	
Loan to:	$	
TOTAL OUT:	$	

PIGGY BANK Savings Account	
Current Piggy Bank:	$
→+ Money IN:	+ $
– Money OUT:	– $
= New Piggy Bank:	= $

Starting Total	$
+ TOTAL IN	+ $
– TOTAL OUT	– $
= New TOTAL put at top of next journal	= $

Breakdown of Your Expenses WEEK:	
MONEY OUT:	
Toys/Video Games/Apps:	$
	$
	$
	$
	$
	$
TOTAL Toys/Video Games/Apps:	$
Food/Beverage:	$
	$
	$
	$
	$
TOTAL Food/Beverage:	$
Entertainment:	$
	$
	$
	$
	$
	$
TOTAL Entertainment:	$
Personal Items:	$
	$
	$
	$
	$
TOTAL Personal Items:	$
For School:	$
	$
TOTAL School:	$
For Car:	$
	$
TOTAL Car:	$
OTHER:	$
	$
	$
	$
TOTAL Other:	$

The Piggy Banker Money Journal   Week: _____

Starting TOTAL: Spending Account	$
MONEY IN:	
Allowance	$
Gift	$
Job	$
Other:	$
TOTAL IN:	$
MONEY OUT:	
Piggy Bank Deposit	$ →
Toys/Video Games/Apps	$
Food/Beverage	$
Entertainment	$
Personal Items	$
For School	$
For Car	$
Other	$
SHARE/Donate:	$
Loan to:	$
TOTAL OUT:	$

PIGGY BANK Savings Account	
Current Piggy Bank:	$
→+ Money IN:	+ $
- Money OUT:	− $
= New Piggy Bank:	= $

Starting Total	$
+ TOTAL IN	+ $
− TOTAL OUT	− $
= New TOTAL put at top of next journal	= $

Breakdown of Your Expenses WEEK:	
MONEY OUT:	
Toys/Video Games/Apps:	$
	$
	$
	$
	$
	$
TOTAL Toys/Video Games/Apps:	$
Food/Beverage:	$
	$
	$
	$
	$
TOTAL Food/Beverage:	$
Entertainment:	$
	$
	$
	$
	$
	$
TOTAL Entertainment:	$
Personal Items:	$
	$
	$
	$
	$
TOTAL Personal Items:	$
For School:	$
	$
TOTAL School:	$
For Car:	$
	$
TOTAL Car:	$
OTHER:	$
	$
	$
	$
TOTAL Other:	$

The Piggy Banker Money Journal   Week: _____

Starting TOTAL: Spending Account	$		PIGGY BANK Savings Account		
MONEY IN:			Current Piggy Bank:	$	
Allowance	$				
Gift	$				
Job	$				
Other:	$				
TOTAL IN:	$				
MONEY OUT:					
Piggy Bank Deposit	$	→	→+ Money IN:	+ $	
Toys/Video Games/Apps	$				
Food/Beverage	$		– Money OUT:	– $	
Entertainment	$				
Personal Items	$				
For School	$				
For Car	$				
Other	$				
SHARE/Donate:	$				
Loan to:	$				
TOTAL OUT:	$		= New Piggy Bank:	= $	

Starting Total	$
+ TOTAL IN	+ $
– TOTAL OUT	– $
= New TOTAL put at top of next journal	= $

Breakdown of Your Expenses WEEK:	
MONEY OUT:	
Toys/Video Games/Apps:	$
	$
	$
	$
	$
	$
TOTAL Toys/Video Games/Apps:	$
Food/Beverage:	$
	$
	$
	$
	$
TOTAL Food/Beverage:	$
Entertainment:	$
	$
	$
	$
	$
	$
TOTAL Entertainment:	$
Personal Items:	$
	$
	$
	$
	$
TOTAL Personal Items:	$
For School:	$
	$
TOTAL School:	$
For Car:	$
	$
TOTAL Car:	$
OTHER:	$
	$
	$
	$
TOTAL Other:	$

The Piggy Banker Money Journal   Week: _____

Starting TOTAL: Spending Account	$

MONEY IN:	
Allowance	$
Gift	$
Job	$
Other:	$
TOTAL IN:	$

MONEY OUT:	
Piggy Bank Deposit	$ →
Toys/Video Games/Apps	$
Food/Beverage	$
Entertainment	$
Personal Items	$
For School	$
For Car	$
Other	$
SHARE/Donate:	$
Loan to:	$
TOTAL OUT:	$

PIGGY BANK Savings Account	
Current Piggy Bank:	$
→+ Money IN:	+ $
- Money OUT:	- $
= New Piggy Bank:	= $

Starting Total	$
+ TOTAL IN	+ $
- TOTAL OUT	- $
= New TOTAL put at top of next journal	= $

Breakdown of Your Expenses WEEK:	
MONEY OUT:	
Toys/Video Games/Apps:	$
	$
	$
	$
	$
	$
TOTAL Toys/Video Games/Apps:	$
Food/Beverage:	$
	$
	$
	$
	$
TOTAL Food/Beverage:	$
Entertainment:	$
	$
	$
	$
	$
	$
TOTAL Entertainment:	$
Personal Items:	$
	$
	$
	$
	$
TOTAL Personal Items:	$
For School:	$
	$
TOTAL School:	$
For Car:	$
	$
TOTAL Car:	$
OTHER:	$
	$
	$
	$
TOTAL Other:	$

The Piggy Banker Money Journal   Week: _____

Starting TOTAL: Spending Account	$
MONEY IN:	
Allowance	$
Gift	$
Job	$
Other:	$
TOTAL IN:	$
MONEY OUT:	
Piggy Bank Deposit	$ →
Toys/Video Games/Apps	$
Food/Beverage	$
Entertainment	$
Personal Items	$
For School	$
For Car	$
Other	$
SHARE/Donate:	$
Loan to:	$
TOTAL OUT:	$

PIGGY BANK Savings Account	
Current Piggy Bank:	$
→+ Money IN:	+ $
- Money OUT:	− $
= New Piggy Bank:	= $

Starting Total	$
+ TOTAL IN	+ $
− TOTAL OUT	− $
= New TOTAL put at top of next journal	= $

Breakdown of Your Expenses WEEK:	
MONEY OUT:	
Toys/Video Games/Apps:	$
	$
	$
	$
	$
	$
TOTAL Toys/Video Games/Apps:	$
Food/Beverage:	$
	$
	$
	$
	$
TOTAL Food/Beverage:	$
Entertainment:	$
	$
	$
	$
	$
	$
TOTAL Entertainment:	$
Personal Items:	$
	$
	$
	$
	$
TOTAL Personal Items:	$
For School:	$
	$
TOTAL School:	$
For Car:	$
	$
TOTAL Car:	$
OTHER:	$
	$
	$
	$
TOTAL Other:	$

The Piggy Banker Money Journal   Week: _____

Starting TOTAL: Spending Account	$

MONEY IN:	
Allowance	$
Gift	$
Job	$
Other:	$
TOTAL IN:	$

MONEY OUT:	
Piggy Bank Deposit	$ →
Toys/Video Games/Apps	$
Food/Beverage	$
Entertainment	$
Personal Items	$
For School	$
For Car	$
Other	$
SHARE/Donate:	$
Loan to:	$
TOTAL OUT:	$

PIGGY BANK Savings Account	
Current Piggy Bank:	$
→+ Money IN:	+ $
- Money OUT:	- $
= New Piggy Bank:	= $

Starting Total	$
+ TOTAL IN	+ $
- TOTAL OUT	- $
= New TOTAL put at top of next journal	= $

Breakdown of Your Expenses WEEK:	
MONEY OUT:	
Toys/Video Games/Apps:	$
	$
	$
	$
	$
	$
TOTAL Toys/Video Games/Apps:	$
Food/Beverage:	$
	$
	$
	$
	$
TOTAL Food/Beverage:	$
Entertainment:	$
	$
	$
	$
	$
	$
TOTAL Entertainment:	$
Personal Items:	$
	$
	$
	$
	$
TOTAL Personal Items:	$
For School:	$
	$
TOTAL School:	$
For Car:	$
	$
TOTAL Car:	$
OTHER:	$
	$
	$
	$
TOTAL Other:	$

The Piggy Banker Money Journal   Week: _____

			PIGGY BANK Savings Account	
Starting TOTAL: Spending Account	**$**			
MONEY IN:			Current Piggy Bank:	**$**
Allowance	$			
Gift	$			
Job	$			
Other:	$			
TOTAL IN:	**$**			
MONEY OUT:				
Piggy Bank Deposit	$	→	→+ Money IN:	+ $
Toys/Video Games/Apps	$			
Food/Beverage	$		- Money OUT:	− $
Entertainment	$			
Personal Items	$			
For School	$			
For Car	$			
Other	$			
SHARE/Donate:	$			
Loan to:	$		**= New Piggy Bank:**	**= $**
TOTAL OUT:	**$**			

Starting Total	**$**
+ TOTAL IN	**+ $**
− TOTAL OUT	**− $**
= New TOTAL put at top of next journal	**= $**

Breakdown of Your Expenses WEEK:	
MONEY OUT:	
Toys/Video Games/Apps:	$
	$
	$
	$
	$
	$
TOTAL Toys/Video Games/Apps:	$
Food/Beverage:	$
	$
	$
	$
	$
TOTAL Food/Beverage:	$
Entertainment:	$
	$
	$
	$
	$
	$
TOTAL Entertainment:	$
Personal Items:	$
	$
	$
	$
	$
TOTAL Personal Items:	$
For School:	$
	$
TOTAL School:	$
For Car:	$
	$
TOTAL Car:	$
OTHER:	$
	$
	$
	$
TOTAL Other:	$

The Piggy Banker Money Journal   Week: _____

Starting TOTAL: Spending Account	$
MONEY IN:	
Allowance	$
Gift	$
Job	$
Other:	$
TOTAL IN:	$
MONEY OUT:	
Piggy Bank Deposit	$ →
Toys/Video Games/Apps	$
Food/Beverage	$
Entertainment	$
Personal Items	$
For School	$
For Car	$
Other	$
SHARE/Donate:	$
Loan to:	$
TOTAL OUT:	$

PIGGY BANK Savings Account	
Current Piggy Bank:	$
→+ Money IN:	+ $
- Money OUT:	_ $
= New Piggy Bank:	= $

Starting Total	$
+ TOTAL IN	+ $
- TOTAL OUT	- $
= New TOTAL put at top of next journal	= $

Breakdown of Your Expenses WEEK:	
MONEY OUT:	
Toys/Video Games/Apps:	$
	$
	$
	$
	$
	$
TOTAL Toys/Video Games/Apps:	$
Food/Beverage:	$
	$
	$
	$
	$
TOTAL Food/Beverage:	$
Entertainment:	$
	$
	$
	$
	$
	$
TOTAL Entertainment:	$
Personal Items:	$
	$
	$
	$
	$
TOTAL Personal Items:	$
For School:	$
	$
TOTAL School:	$
For Car:	$
	$
TOTAL Car:	$
OTHER:	$
	$
	$
	$
TOTAL Other:	$

The Piggy Banker Money Journal   Week: _____

Starting TOTAL: Spending Account	$
MONEY IN:	
Allowance	$
Gift	$
Job	$
Other:	$
TOTAL IN:	$
MONEY OUT:	
Piggy Bank Deposit	$ →
Toys/Video Games/Apps	$
Food/Beverage	$
Entertainment	$
Personal Items	$
For School	$
For Car	$
Other	$
SHARE/Donate:	$
Loan to:	$
TOTAL OUT:	$

PIGGY BANK Savings Account	
Current Piggy Bank:	$
→+ Money IN:	+ $
− Money OUT:	− $
= New Piggy Bank:	= $

Starting Total	$
+ TOTAL IN	+ $
− TOTAL OUT	− $
= New TOTAL put at top of next journal	= $

Breakdown of Your Expenses WEEK:	
MONEY OUT:	
Toys/Video Games/Apps:	$
	$
	$
	$
	$
	$
TOTAL Toys/Video Games/Apps:	$
Food/Beverage:	$
	$
	$
	$
	$
TOTAL Food/Beverage:	$
Entertainment:	$
	$
	$
	$
	$
	$
TOTAL Entertainment:	$
Personal Items:	$
	$
	$
	$
	$
TOTAL Personal Items:	$
For School:	$
	$
TOTAL School:	$
For Car:	$
	$
TOTAL Car:	$
OTHER:	$
	$
	$
	$
TOTAL Other:	$

The Piggy Banker Money Journal   Week: _____

Starting TOTAL: Spending Account	$		PIGGY BANK Savings Account	
MONEY IN:			Current Piggy Bank:	$
Allowance	$			
Gift	$			
Job	$			
Other:	$			
TOTAL IN:	$			
MONEY OUT:				
Piggy Bank Deposit	$	→	→+ Money IN:	+ $
Toys/Video Games/Apps	$			
Food/Beverage	$		− Money OUT:	− $
Entertainment	$			
Personal Items	$			
For School	$			
For Car	$			
Other	$			
SHARE/Donate:	$			
Loan to:	$		= New Piggy Bank:	= $
TOTAL OUT:	$			

Starting Total	$
+ TOTAL IN	+ $
− TOTAL OUT	− $
= New TOTAL put at top of next journal	= $

Breakdown of Your Expenses WEEK:	
MONEY OUT:	
Toys/Video Games/Apps:	$
	$
	$
	$
	$
	$
TOTAL Toys/Video Games/Apps:	$
Food/Beverage:	$
	$
	$
	$
	$
TOTAL Food/Beverage:	$
Entertainment:	$
	$
	$
	$
	$
	$
TOTAL Entertainment:	$
Personal Items:	$
	$
	$
	$
	$
TOTAL Personal Items:	$
For School:	$
	$
TOTAL School:	$
For Car:	$
	$
TOTAL Car:	$
OTHER:	$
	$
	$
	$
TOTAL Other:	$

The Piggy Banker Money Journal   Week: _____

Starting TOTAL: Spending Account	$

MONEY IN:	
Allowance	$
Gift	$
Job	$
Other:	$
TOTAL IN:	$

MONEY OUT:	
Piggy Bank Deposit	$ →
Toys/Video Games/Apps	$
Food/Beverage	$
Entertainment	$
Personal Items	$
For School	$
For Car	$
Other	$
SHARE/Donate:	$
Loan to:	$
TOTAL OUT:	$

PIGGY BANK Savings Account	
Current Piggy Bank:	$
→+ Money IN:	+ $
– Money OUT:	– $
= New Piggy Bank:	= $

Starting Total	$
+ TOTAL IN	+ $
– TOTAL OUT	– $
= New TOTAL put at top of next journal	= $

Breakdown of Your Expenses WEEK:	
MONEY OUT:	
Toys/Video Games/Apps:	$
	$
	$
	$
	$
	$
TOTAL Toys/Video Games/Apps:	$
Food/Beverage:	$
	$
	$
	$
	$
TOTAL Food/Beverage:	$
Entertainment:	$
	$
	$
	$
	$
	$
TOTAL Entertainment:	$
Personal Items:	$
	$
	$
	$
	$
TOTAL Personal Items:	$
For School:	$
	$
TOTAL School:	$
For Car:	$
	$
TOTAL Car:	$
OTHER:	$
	$
	$
	$
TOTAL Other:	$

The Piggy Banker Money Journal   Week: _____

Starting TOTAL: Spending Account	$		PIGGY BANK Savings Account	
MONEY IN:			Current Piggy Bank:	$
Allowance	$			
Gift	$			
Job	$			
Other:	$			
TOTAL IN:	$			
MONEY OUT:				
Piggy Bank Deposit	$ →		→+ Money IN:	+ $
Toys/Video Games/Apps	$			
Food/Beverage	$		- Money OUT:	− $
Entertainment	$			
Personal Items	$			
For School	$			
For Car	$			
Other	$			
SHARE/Donate:	$			
Loan to:	$		= New Piggy Bank:	= $
TOTAL OUT:	$			

Starting Total	$
+ TOTAL IN	+ $
− TOTAL OUT	− $
= New TOTAL put at top of next journal	= $

Breakdown of Your Expenses WEEK:	
MONEY OUT:	
Toys/Video Games/Apps:	$
	$
	$
	$
	$
	$
TOTAL Toys/Video Games/Apps:	$
Food/Beverage:	$
	$
	$
	$
	$
TOTAL Food/Beverage:	$
Entertainment:	$
	$
	$
	$
	$
	$
TOTAL Entertainment:	$
Personal Items:	$
	$
	$
	$
	$
TOTAL Personal Items:	$
For School:	$
	$
TOTAL School:	$
For Car:	$
	$
TOTAL Car:	$
OTHER:	$
	$
	$
	$
TOTAL Other:	$

The Piggy Banker Money Journal   Week: _____

Starting TOTAL: Spending Account	$
MONEY IN:	
Allowance	$
Gift	$
Job	$
Other:	$
TOTAL IN:	$
MONEY OUT:	
Piggy Bank Deposit	$ →
Toys/Video Games/Apps	$
Food/Beverage	$
Entertainment	$
Personal Items	$
For School	$
For Car	$
Other	$
SHARE/Donate:	$
Loan to:	$
TOTAL OUT:	$

PIGGY BANK Savings Account	
Current Piggy Bank:	$
→ + Money IN:	+ $
- Money OUT:	_ $
= New Piggy Bank:	= $

Starting Total	$
+ TOTAL IN	+ $
- TOTAL OUT	- $
= New TOTAL put at top of next journal	= $

Breakdown of Your Expenses WEEK:	
MONEY OUT:	
Toys/Video Games/Apps:	$
	$
	$
	$
	$
	$
TOTAL Toys/Video Games/Apps:	$
Food/Beverage:	$
	$
	$
	$
	$
TOTAL Food/Beverage:	$
Entertainment:	$
	$
	$
	$
	$
	$
TOTAL Entertainment:	$
Personal Items:	$
	$
	$
	$
	$
TOTAL Personal Items:	$
For School:	$
	$
TOTAL School:	$
For Car:	$
	$
TOTAL Car:	$
OTHER:	$
	$
	$
	$
TOTAL Other:	$

The Piggy Banker Money Journal   Week: _____

Starting TOTAL: Spending Account	$
MONEY IN:	
Allowance	$
Gift	$
Job	$
Other:	$
TOTAL IN:	$
MONEY OUT:	
Piggy Bank Deposit	$ →
Toys/Video Games/Apps	$
Food/Beverage	$
Entertainment	$
Personal Items	$
For School	$
For Car	$
Other	$
SHARE/Donate:	$
Loan to:	$
TOTAL OUT:	$

PIGGY BANK Savings Account	
Current Piggy Bank:	$
→+ Money IN:	+ $
- Money OUT:	− $
= New Piggy Bank:	= $

Starting Total	$
+ TOTAL IN	+ $
− TOTAL OUT	− $
= New TOTAL put at top of next journal	= $

Breakdown of Your Expenses WEEK:	
MONEY OUT:	
Toys/Video Games/Apps:	$
	$
	$
	$
	$
	$
TOTAL Toys/Video Games/Apps:	$
Food/Beverage:	$
	$
	$
	$
	$
TOTAL Food/Beverage:	$
Entertainment:	$
	$
	$
	$
	$
	$
TOTAL Entertainment:	$
Personal Items:	$
	$
	$
	$
	$
TOTAL Personal Items:	$
For School:	$
	$
TOTAL School:	$
For Car:	$
	$
TOTAL Car:	$
OTHER:	$
	$
	$
	$
TOTAL Other:	$

The Piggy Banker Money Journal   Week: _____

Starting TOTAL: Spending Account	$
MONEY IN:	
Allowance	$
Gift	$
Job	$
Other:	$
TOTAL IN:	$
MONEY OUT:	
Piggy Bank Deposit	$ →
Toys/Video Games/Apps	$
Food/Beverage	$
Entertainment	$
Personal Items	$
For School	$
For Car	$
Other	$
SHARE/Donate:	$
Loan to:	$
TOTAL OUT:	$

PIGGY BANK Savings Account	
Current Piggy Bank:	$
→ + Money IN:	+ $
- Money OUT:	_ $
= New Piggy Bank:	= $

Starting Total	$
+ TOTAL IN	+ $
- TOTAL OUT	- $
= New TOTAL put at top of next journal	= $

Breakdown of Your Expenses WEEK:	
MONEY OUT:	
Toys/Video Games/Apps:	$
	$
	$
	$
	$
	$
TOTAL Toys/Video Games/Apps:	$
Food/Beverage:	$
	$
	$
	$
	$
TOTAL Food/Beverage:	$
Entertainment:	$
	$
	$
	$
	$
	$
TOTAL Entertainment:	$
Personal Items:	$
	$
	$
	$
	$
TOTAL Personal Items:	$
For School:	$
	$
TOTAL School:	$
For Car:	$
	$
TOTAL Car:	$
OTHER:	$
	$
	$
	$
TOTAL Other:	$

The Piggy Banker Money Journal   Week: _____

Starting TOTAL: Spending Account	$
MONEY IN:	
Allowance	$
Gift	$
Job	$
Other:	$
TOTAL IN:	$
MONEY OUT:	
Piggy Bank Deposit	$ →
Toys/Video Games/Apps	$
Food/Beverage	$
Entertainment	$
Personal Items	$
For School	$
For Car	$
Other	$
SHARE/Donate:	$
Loan to:	$
TOTAL OUT:	$

PIGGY BANK Savings Account	
Current Piggy Bank:	$
→+ Money IN:	+ $
- Money OUT:	_ $
= New Piggy Bank:	= $

Starting Total	$
+ TOTAL IN	+ $
- TOTAL OUT	- $
= New TOTAL put at top of next journal	= $

Breakdown of Your Expenses WEEK:	
MONEY OUT:	
Toys/Video Games/Apps:	$
	$
	$
	$
	$
	$
TOTAL Toys/Video Games/Apps:	$
Food/Beverage:	$
	$
	$
	$
	$
TOTAL Food/Beverage:	$
Entertainment:	$
	$
	$
	$
	$
	$
TOTAL Entertainment:	$
Personal Items:	$
	$
	$
	$
	$
TOTAL Personal Items:	$
For School:	$
	$
TOTAL School:	$
For Car:	$
	$
TOTAL Car:	$
OTHER:	$
	$
	$
	$
TOTAL Other:	$

The Piggy Banker Money Journal

Week: _____

Starting TOTAL: Spending Account	$
MONEY IN:	
Allowance	$
Gift	$
Job	$
Other:	$
TOTAL IN:	$
MONEY OUT:	
Piggy Bank Deposit	$ →
Toys/Video Games/Apps	$
Food/Beverage	$
Entertainment	$
Personal Items	$
For School	$
For Car	$
Other	$
SHARE/Donate:	$
Loan to:	$
TOTAL OUT:	$

PIGGY BANK Savings Account	
Current Piggy Bank:	$
→+ Money IN:	+ $
- Money OUT:	_ $
= New Piggy Bank:	= $

Starting Total	$
+ TOTAL IN	+ $
- TOTAL OUT	- $
= New TOTAL put at top of next journal	= $

Breakdown of Your Expenses WEEK:	
MONEY OUT:	
Toys/Video Games/Apps:	$
	$
	$
	$
	$
	$
TOTAL Toys/Video Games/Apps:	$
Food/Beverage:	$
	$
	$
	$
	$
TOTAL Food/Beverage:	$
Entertainment:	$
	$
	$
	$
	$
	$
TOTAL Entertainment:	$
Personal Items:	$
	$
	$
	$
	$
TOTAL Personal Items:	$
For School:	$
	$
TOTAL School:	$
For Car:	$
	$
TOTAL Car:	$
OTHER:	$
	$
	$
	$
TOTAL Other:	$

The Piggy Banker Money Journal   Week: _____

Starting TOTAL: Spending Account	$
MONEY IN:	
Allowance	$
Gift	$
Job	$
Other:	$
TOTAL IN:	$
MONEY OUT:	
Piggy Bank Deposit	$ →
Toys/Video Games/Apps	$
Food/Beverage	$
Entertainment	$
Personal Items	$
For School	$
For Car	$
Other	$
SHARE/Donate:	$
Loan to:	$
TOTAL OUT:	$

PIGGY BANK Savings Account	
Current Piggy Bank:	$
→+ Money IN:	+ $
- Money OUT:	− $
= New Piggy Bank:	**= $**

Starting Total	$
+ TOTAL IN	+ $
− TOTAL OUT	− $
= New TOTAL put at top of next journal	= $

Breakdown of Your Expenses WEEK:	
MONEY OUT:	
Toys/Video Games/Apps:	$
	$
	$
	$
	$
	$
TOTAL Toys/Video Games/Apps:	$
Food/Beverage:	$
	$
	$
	$
	$
TOTAL Food/Beverage:	$
Entertainment:	$
	$
	$
	$
	$
	$
TOTAL Entertainment:	$
Personal Items:	$
	$
	$
	$
	$
TOTAL Personal Items:	$
For School:	$
	$
TOTAL School:	$
For Car:	$
	$
TOTAL Car:	$
OTHER:	$
	$
	$
	$
TOTAL Other:	$

The Piggy Banker Money Journal   Week: _____

Starting TOTAL: Spending Account	$
MONEY IN:	
Allowance	$
Gift	$
Job	$
Other:	$
TOTAL IN:	$
MONEY OUT:	
Piggy Bank Deposit	$ →
Toys/Video Games/Apps	$
Food/Beverage	$
Entertainment	$
Personal Items	$
For School	$
For Car	$
Other	$
SHARE/Donate:	$
Loan to:	$
TOTAL OUT:	$

PIGGY BANK Savings Account	
Current Piggy Bank:	$
→+ Money IN:	+ $
- Money OUT:	− $
= New Piggy Bank:	= $

Starting Total	$
+ TOTAL IN	+ $
− TOTAL OUT	− $
= New TOTAL put at top of next journal	= $

Breakdown of Your Expenses WEEK:	
MONEY OUT:	
Toys/Video Games/Apps:	$
	$
	$
	$
	$
	$
TOTAL Toys/Video Games/Apps:	$
Food/Beverage:	$
	$
	$
	$
	$
TOTAL Food/Beverage:	$
Entertainment:	$
	$
	$
	$
	$
	$
TOTAL Entertainment:	$
Personal Items:	$
	$
	$
	$
	$
TOTAL Personal Items:	$
For School:	$
	$
TOTAL School:	$
For Car:	$
	$
TOTAL Car:	$
OTHER:	$
	$
	$
	$
TOTAL Other:	$

The Piggy Banker Money Journal   Week: _____

Starting TOTAL: Spending Account	$		PIGGY BANK Savings Account	
MONEY IN:			Current Piggy Bank:	$
Allowance	$			
Gift	$			
Job	$			
Other:	$			
TOTAL IN:	$			
MONEY OUT:				
Piggy Bank Deposit	$ →		→+ Money IN:	+ $
Toys/Video Games/Apps	$			
Food/Beverage	$		– Money OUT:	– $
Entertainment	$			
Personal Items	$			
For School	$			
For Car	$			
Other	$			
SHARE/Donate:	$			
Loan to:	$		= New Piggy Bank:	= $
TOTAL OUT:	$			

Starting Total	$
+ TOTAL IN	+ $
– TOTAL OUT	– $
= New TOTAL put at top of next journal	= $

Breakdown of Your Expenses WEEK:	
MONEY OUT:	
Toys/Video Games/Apps:	$
	$
	$
	$
	$
	$
TOTAL Toys/Video Games/Apps:	$
Food/Beverage:	$
	$
	$
	$
	$
TOTAL Food/Beverage:	$
Entertainment:	$
	$
	$
	$
	$
	$
TOTAL Entertainment:	$
Personal Items:	$
	$
	$
	$
	$
TOTAL Personal Items:	$
For School:	$
	$
TOTAL School:	$
For Car:	$
	$
TOTAL Car:	$
OTHER:	$
	$
	$
	$
TOTAL Other:	$

The Piggy Banker Money Journal   Week: _____

Starting TOTAL: Spending Account	$
MONEY IN:	
Allowance	$
Gift	$
Job	$
Other:	$
TOTAL IN:	$
MONEY OUT:	
Piggy Bank Deposit	$ →
Toys/Video Games/Apps	$
Food/Beverage	$
Entertainment	$
Personal Items	$
For School	$
For Car	$
Other	$
SHARE/Donate:	$
Loan to:	$
TOTAL OUT:	$

PIGGY BANK Savings Account	
Current Piggy Bank:	$
→+ Money IN:	+ $
– Money OUT:	– $
= New Piggy Bank:	**= $**

Starting Total	$
+ TOTAL IN	+ $
– TOTAL OUT	– $
= New TOTAL put at top of next journal	= $

PIGGY BANKER WISH LIST

Don't forget to do a check-in and compare the cost of your Wish List item to how much money you currently have in your spending account or saved in your Piggy Bank. Are you getting closer?

COST:

PIGGY BANKER WISH LIST

Don't forget to do a check-in and compare the cost of your Wish List item to how much money you currently have in your spending account or saved in your Piggy Bank. Are you getting closer?

COST:

PIGGY BANKER WISH LIST

Don't forget to do a check-in and compare the cost of your Wish List item to how much money you currently have in your spending account or saved in your Piggy Bank. Are you getting closer?

COST:

Raise Creative Investors

PIGGY BANKER WISH LIST

Don't forget to do a check-in and compare the cost of your Wish List item to how much money you currently have in your spending account or saved in your Piggy Bank. Are you getting closer?

COST:

PIGGY BANKER WISH LIST

Don't forget to do a check-in and compare the cost of your Wish List item to how much money you currently have in your spending account or saved in your Piggy Bank. Are you getting closer?

COST:

PIGGY BANKER WISH LIST

Don't forget to do a check-in and compare the cost of your Wish List item to how much money you currently have in your spending account or saved in your Piggy Bank. Are you getting closer?

COST:

PIGGY BANKER WISH LIST

Don't forget to do a check-in and compare the cost of your Wish List item to how much money you currently have in your spending account or saved in your Piggy Bank. Are you getting closer?

COST:

PIGGY BANKER WISH LIST

Don't forget to do a check-in and compare the cost of your Wish List item to how much money you currently have in your spending account or saved in your Piggy Bank. Are you getting closer?

COST:

PIGGY BANKER WISH LIST

Don't forget to do a check-in and compare the cost of your Wish List item to how much money you currently have in your spending account or saved in your Piggy Bank. Are you getting closer?

COST:

PIGGY BANKER WISH LIST

Don't forget to do a check-in and compare the cost of your Wish List item to how much money you currently have in your spending account or saved in your Piggy Bank. Are you getting closer?

COST:

PIGGY BANKER WISH LIST

Don't forget to do a check-in and compare the cost of your Wish List item to how much money you currently have in your spending account or saved in your Piggy Bank. Are you getting closer?

COST:

The Piggy Banker

A Raise Creative Investors Money Journal

Congratulations on taking this step toward improving on your financial literacy and becoming more aware of how you spend and save your money. Make this just your first step, of many to follow, on your journey to becoming better educated on all financial matters. You will have many important financial decisions to make in the future, including how to deal with the debt you may face from your college education, what type of mortgage to take out to buy your future home, whether you should lease or buy a car, and how to save for your retirement. The better educated on and comfortable with financial matters you are, the better decisions you will make, and in the long run, the better off you will be financially.

Visit our website **http://RaiseCreativeInvestors.com** for more financial lessons and encourage family discussions around money matters to continue to help boost your financial literacy.

Sincerely, Your Piggy Banker

www.ingramcontent.com/pod-product-compliance
Lightning Source LLC
Chambersburg PA
CBHW051347200326
41521CB00014B/2506